Post-Industrial Development in East Asia

Min-Hua Chiang

Post-Industrial Development in East Asia

Taiwan and South Korea in Comparison

palgrave
macmillan

Min-Hua Chiang
East Asian Institute
National University of Singapore
Singapore, Singapore

ISBN 978-981-13-0273-2 ISBN 978-981-13-0274-9 (eBook)
https://doi.org/10.1007/978-981-13-0274-9

Library of Congress Control Number: 2018942744

Cover illustration: Modern building window © saulgranda/Getty

Printed on acid-free paper

This Palgrave Pivot imprint is published by the registered company Springer Nature Singapore Pte Ltd. part of Springer Nature.
The registered company address is: 152 Beach Road, #21-01/04 Gateway East, Singapore 189721, Singapore

Contents

List of Figures

List of Tables

CHAPTER 1

Introduction

Abstract This introductory chapter sets the scene for the remainder of the book and briefly reviews the main ideas of analysis in each chapter. It compares Taiwan and South Korea's economic conditions after World War II and after the Asian financial crisis. The *problematique* appears from the different economic performance of Taiwan and South Korea during these two different periods. The theoretical debates about both countries' post-war economic development are discussed and used as references to examine Taiwan and South Korea's economic development after they have achieved post-war industrialization.

Keywords Post-war economic development • Post-industrial development • Developmental state • Entrepreneurship • The US-led modernization project

What happened to Taiwan's and South Korea's economies after having achieved successful post-war industrialization? The success of economic development after World War II (WWII) in both countries is well known but their development after post-war industrialization has not yet been comprehensively recorded and compared. Did Taiwan's and South Korea's economies continue to grow not only in terms of quantity but also in terms of quality? If so, what are the contributing factors behind their post-industrial economic development? If not, what made these two economies

M.-H. Chiang, *Post-Industrial Development in East Asia*,
https://doi.org/10.1007/978-981-13-0274-9_1

stop progressing? This book purports to investigate and compare the economic development experiences in both Taiwan and South Korea in the most recent two decades. Through analyzing and comparing these two empirical cases, the book aims to incorporate additional factors into the explanatory paradigms in development theories. In the process, this book also attempts to highlight and synthesize some major features of these two economies' development experiences in modern history.

This chapter sets the scene for the remainder of the book by providing the background information about Taiwan's and South Korea's development after WWII. We will firstly review the similar and different development paths in Taiwan and South Korea after WWII. Second, the major theories explaining Taiwan's and South Korea's post-war economic development are discussed. Third, we compare Taiwan's and South Korea's economic development after the Asian financial crisis (AFC). Comparison of the major economic indicators in these two countries in the last two decades allows for subsequent summary of the main development differences after the AFC. The research questions and research methods are addressed in the final section of the chapter.

Similar Post-War Development Paths

Taiwan and South Korea are widely considered as two successful economic development models after WWII. In less than two decades after the war, both had transformed from agricultural nations to major global manufacturers. Their successful industrialization from light to heavy industries supported their high economic growth rates for more than three decades since the 1960s except during the oil crises in 1973 and 1979 (Fig. 1.1). The gross domestic product (GDP) per capita in Taiwan increased from a mere US$152 in 1961 to US$9092 by 1991. During the same period, South Korea's GDP per capita also augmented from a mere US$91.5 to US$7523 (IMF 2015). In addition, the successful industrialization allowed the manufacturing sector to provide job opportunities for the mass of laborers released from the agricultural sector. As a result, tens of millions of people were quickly pulled out of poverty. With the economic advancement, these two US-aid recipients in the 1950s and 1960s quickly transformed into aid donors and important investors, particularly in Asia since the early 1990s.

Taiwan and South Korea had similar conditions for development at the initial stage. Both had been colonized by Japan before and during the

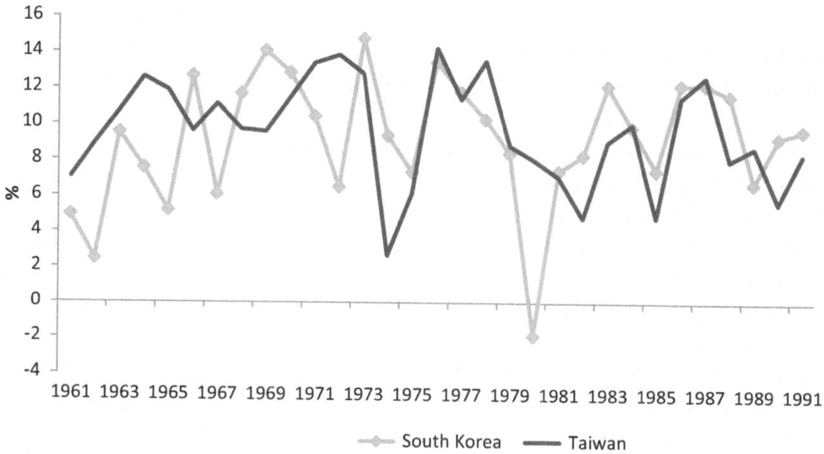

Fig. 1.1 Taiwan and South Korea's annual economic growth rates 1961–1991. Source: IMF (2015)

WWII, and had very limited natural resources and endowment for development. After WWII, both faced potential armed conflict with Communist regimes. In general, the evolution of these two countries' post-war development paths can be categorized into three major stages. First, US aid played an important role in Taiwan's and South Korea's post-war economic recovery during the 1950s. The aid financed their imports of food and consumption goods after the war as well as the governments' fiscal deficits. Domestic economy would not be easily stabilized without US aid. Although defense expenditure was large, it would be even larger if there had not been for US military aid. The US military intervention in both the Taiwan Strait and the Korean Peninsula further helped Taiwan and South Korea prevent military invasion from the communist regimes. The sense of security encouraged private investment and bolstered confidence of the two populations.

Second, the governments in these two economies were strongly committed to economic development as a national goal. Both had engaged in a short period of import-substitute industrialization before the implementation of the export expansion strategy that successfully drove their post-war industrialization. Import-substitute industrialization was carried out through strict quantitative restrictions on imports. The industrialization was further promoted by highly subsidized credit and selective foreign exchange licensing allocations. However, the industrial output was not competitive on the world market and domestic demand for the industrial output was exhausted few years later. Import substitution was soon replaced by the export-led growth in labor-intensive consumer goods manufacturing (Adelman 1999). The US and Japan were the two essential pillars in supporting Taiwan's and Korea's export expansion. Japan acted as the key supplier of capital equipment to Taiwanese and South Korean manufacturers while the US was the largest destination market for manufactured final goods in both countries.

Finally, both countries have embarked on a broad range of economic liberalization measures since the 1980s. In response to the growing protectionism from the Western countries, import tariffs were substantially reduced in Taiwan and South Korea. Control over financial sectors, foreign exchange rates, interest rates, and investment were progressively deregulated. The market liberalization did not result in economic volatility as some conservative politicians had expected. Instead, both economies continued to expand at remarkable rates until the AFC in 1997.

Some Differences

Despite their similarities in economic performance and policy measures, macroeconomic figures reveal some differences between the two countries as indicated in Table 1.1. First of all, Taiwan's GDP per capita was higher than that of South Korea after the war. This could be reasoned by South Korea's lag in industrialization at the initial stage of post-war development (Hattori and Sato 1997). Indeed, Taiwan's head start in industrialization can be traced back to the Japanese colonial period, in its provision of military goods for Japanese armed forces during WWII. Taiwan's industrial capacity accumulated during the war facilitated its post-war economic recovery. Although Japan also industrialized Korea during the colonial period, most of the factories were located in the North. South Korea lost its industrial power after the Korean Peninsula was divided after 1945.

Second, while Taiwan's economy grew rapidly after the war, it managed to improve income distribution with a fairly stable price level. Korea also improved its income distribution in the course of drastic economic growth before 1970. Nonetheless, its income distribution has been worsening since the 1970s. The low interest rate policy, rapid development of urbanization, and large companies' dominance in business are considered responsible for the enlarging income inequality in South Korea (Yoo 1990).

Table 1.1 Selected macroeconomic indicators in Taiwan and South Korea 1980–1995

		Taiwan	*South Korea*
Economic growth rates (%)	1980	7.3	−1.7
	1985	4.8	7.8
	1990	5.6	9.8
	1995	6.5	9.6
Per capita GDP (US$)	1980	2367.4	1710.8
	1985	3295.1	2457.7
	1990	8178.2	6513.2
	1995	13,076.0	12,340.0
Inflation (%)	1980	19.0	28.7
	1985	−0.2	2.5
	1990	4.1	8.6
	1995	3.7	4.5
Unemployment rate (%)	1980	1.2	5.2
	1985	2.9	4.0
	1990	1.7	2.5
	1995	1.8	2.0
Current account balance (US$ billion)	1980	n/a	−5.3
	1985	9.2	−2.1
	1990	10.9	−2.4
	1995	5.5	−9.8

Source: International Monetary Fund (2015)

In particular, in order to attain economies of scale, the government deliberately concentrated economic power in the hands of a small number of conglomerates. Korea's high inflation rate is also considered an important reason for the wider income inequality (Byun 1993). Unlike South Korea, it was small and medium entreprises (SMEs) that drove Taiwan's export-oriented economic development. Taiwan's SMEs-dominated economic structure was considered indispensable in equalizing income distribution.

Third, although the unemployment rate in South Korea had clearly declined from 7.7 percent in 1964 to 5.2 percent by 1980, it was still relatively higher compared to that in Taiwan. The stability of employment is another contributor to the equal income distribution. Taiwan's low unemployment rates showed that its industrialization successfully absorbed the large labor force from the agricultural sector. In South Korea, its unemployment rates were clearly decreased only after the latter half of the 1980s. One explanation for its relatively higher unemployment rates before the mid-1980s was that South Korea's policy shift toward capital-intensive heavy industries during the 1970s has reduced its demand for the large number of unskilled labors (Kim 1990). In comparison, while developing heavy industries, Taiwan also emphasized on labor-intensive light manufacturing production.

Fourth, it is noteworthy that South Korea relied heavily on international borrowing to finance its investment whereas Taiwan relied more on domestic savings. As a result, Taiwan had a much lower foreign debt burden than South Korea. Taiwan's high interest rate and flat inflation accelerated its capital accumulation. While high interest rate encouraged savings, the lending rates were not high enough to reduce business investment. Although South Korea also adopted a similar high interest rate policy in 1965, it was hard to reconcile with governmental control over private investment through concessionary loans (Scitovsky 1986).

Finally, the external trade balance was different. As mentioned, the successful industrialization allowed Taiwan and South Korea to export large manufactured goods to the Western countries. At the same time, both depended on importing key components from Japan. Owing to the much larger exports of manufactured goods than imports, Taiwan enjoyed constant trade surplus since the 1980s. In contrast, South Korea's annual trade balance had remained in deficit before 1997. Taiwan's gradual development of trade surplus has also contributed to its constant current account surplus. In comparison, South Korea's annual current account had mostly remained in deficit during the 1980s and early 1990s, mainly a result of its constant trade deficit.

Theoretical Explanations

How did these similar and different economic features in both countries contribute to their economic success after WWII? This question has brought many developmental economists into an incessant debate. The neoclassical economists believe that market forces are the engine of economic growth while the developmental state supporters argue the greater role of the governments in guiding the development. Taiwan's and South Korea's post-war economic success also challenged the Marxist view that countries in the periphery are not able to develop due to the asymmetrical power relations with the center and semi-periphery. Below are three major arguments from the literature in explaining Taiwan's and South Korea's post-war industrialization, including private sectors' contribution, appropriate state policies, and the US factor.

Private Enterprises' Contribution to the Economic Boom

Taiwan's export expansion in the 1970s and 1980s was mostly attributed to the efforts of SMEs. In 1985, for example, the 12 largest firms in Taiwan only accounted for 10 percent of exports, the remaining 90 percent was made by the SMEs (Taniura 1992). Strong entrepreneurship, high production flexibility, and high sensitivity to external market demand are often cited as Taiwan SMEs' major strengths for their success (Hu and Schive 1998; Lee and Hsiao 2014; Lin 1998; Wu 2005). Although the Kuomintang (KMT) government did not intentionally nurture SMEs, the business-friendly environment, such as inexpensive labor cost and low inflation rate, had facilitated SMEs' business operations. Unlike in South Korea, the major economic development policies such as export promotion policy did not discriminate among firms of different sizes (Hu and Schive 1998). When many export-oriented foreign companies arrived to invest in Taiwan, many Taiwan SMEs established individual production contracts with them, in particular with American and Japanese firms. These contracts were mostly original equipment manufacturer (OEM) arrangements in which Taiwan SMEs were responsible for producing under the multinational corporations' (MNCs') brand names. During the 1980s, local companies in Taiwan gradually moved from manufacturing computer mice, keyboards, and power supplies to more advanced products, such as motherboards, scanners, and monitors for foreign MNCs (Kraemer et al. 2011). Since the 1990s, with the spike in the global demand for PCs, Taiwanese firms became original design manufacturers (ODM), which allowed the firms to design as well as manufacture for foreign MNCs.

Different from the SME-dominant Taiwanese economy, South Korea's economy grew as a result of leadership by a few colossal enterprises, a family-controlled commercial and industrial combination, called *chaebol*. Korean chaebol development began as early as in the 1950s. In order to secure political support from the private sector, South Korea's first president Syngman Rhee distributed state-controlled resources to certain companies which had close relations with the ruling party. A military government led by Park Chung-hee in the 1960s and 1970s consolidated the partnership between the government and large business groups even further. The Park government provided many incentives, such as preferential banking loans and induced foreign capital to large private firms to spur their production capacity for exports. Compared with other small firms, large companies were able to capitalize on the economies of scale of their production. The government also favored a handful of large firms over a large number of small firms, given the convenience of cooperating with a few business leaders (Chiang 2016). The government's promotion of heavy and chemical industry (HCI) in the 1970s further strengthened its coalition with large companies at the expense of smaller enterprises. At the end of the 1970s, HCIs dominated by a few chaebols accounted for 80 percent of fixed investment and 40 percent of output in the manufacturing sectors (Lim 2003). On the other hand, Korean SMEs have been more focused on the domestic market and less involved in international trade.

Some considered the different entrepreneurship in Taiwan and Korean SMEs as a result of government policy. While the Taiwanese government adopted a policy of supporting enterprise growth by their own efforts, the Korean government selected sectors of industry and enterprises to be fostered. Consequently, Taiwan enterprises have developed an ability to be competitive in the world whereas Korean SMEs are not able to develop their own independent capabilities to compete internationally (Hayashida 1994). One common characteristic of Taiwan's SMEs and Korean chaebols is that they are all family-owned companies. Underlying small business dynamics in Taiwan is the Chinese family style of management. Small entrepreneurs in Taiwan have been alert to profit opportunities. With short-term planning, they act as imitators as well as OEM manufacturers in international subcontracting markets (Yu 2009). On the other hand, Korean chaebols' structure of ownership was based on cross-ownership linkage among affiliated companies. As the distinction between ownership and management was fuzzy, chaebol owners dominated both board of directors and management (Ha and Lee 2007). Unlike Taiwan SMEs' struggle to win orders from foreign MNCs, Korean chaebols often found new business from the government's industrial policies in the domestic economy.

The State Policy

From the statist viewpoint, a strong government is the key to rapid growth as the state's autonomous power would facilitate the national growth strategy and prevent policy distortion due to the disagreement from domestic interest groups (Tsai 1999). The KMT's pro-capitalist nature, the relative absence of military participation in economic policymaking, and the distant relation with local elites reinforced its autonomy in Taiwan (Evens and Pang 1989). Wade argued that both Little and Gustav Ranis' work "largely ignore the promotional role of government after the economic liberalization of 1958–62 and the fiscal incentives to attract foreign investment and the industrial planning on the promotion of industries" (Wade 1990). Those scholars who emphasized the state considered that the exploitation of the comparative advantage in Taiwan as well as in other newly industrializing countries (NIC) was through the governments' industrial planning (Haggard 1990). They emphasized the skilled technocrats of the KMT in moving the island toward industrialization (Ho Samuel P.S. 1987). Scholars who supported the important role of government also found the traditional dependency theory unable to explain Taiwan's economic development. They argued that although Taiwan has been dependent on foreign trade and investment, this dependence did not lead the island's economy to a failure, as dependency theory claimed. In contrast, the influence of foreign economic penetration is essential in understanding Taiwan's post-war economic achievements.

In South Korea, the government's policy was also considered essential for its post-war development (Kim 1991). Since a number of large companies were cultivated by the government, it is argued that South Korea's economy had more government-led character than Taiwan's (Hattori and Sato 1997). In general, the Korean development strategy had four facets: rapid growth orientation, industrialization, export-drive, and high dependency on industrial sectors dominated by large firms (Byun 1993). In the 1960s, the Park Chung-hee government created the economic planning board (EPB) to facilitate the follow-up economic policy implementation. During Park's administration, domestic interest rates were kept below real market prices and loans to private firms were subsidized. In addition, the Park government nationalized the banking system and by 1970 it controlled 96.4 percent of the country's financial assets. The absolute control over the national finance allowed the EPB to distribute resources to areas that the government intended for development. In the 1970s, the government mobilized all institutional and material resources to develop HCI (Li 2002). The threat of the withdrawal of financial assistance was serious for the firms performing under the government's target due to their high debt-to-equity ratio (Minns 2001). Because of the tight control over the domestic politics, the government encountered little challenge from the main classes of the Korean society. The high degree of state autonomy allowed it to mobilize resources to meet its economic planning objectives. In contrast to the state, chaebols did not possess a high degree of autonomy during the unpredictable and political-oriented development process. Hence, it is argued that chaebols were actually used as a tool for the state to pursue the economic development goal (Hundt 2009).

The US Factor

The external influences including US aid at the initial stage of post-war development and the subsequent economic dependence on the US market were also considered indispensable factors for Taiwan's and South Korea's post-war economic success. Under what Berger called "the US-led modernization project", a group of countries in Asia was successfully transformed into modern capitalist countries since the Cold War era. The modernization project centered on the state-guided national development in these countries was actually associated with the US security interests against the communist regimes between the 1940s and the 1970s (Berger 2004).

Among the Asian countries, Japan was the first economy to develop in the post-war era under the US umbrella. The US hoped that its aid in revitalizing the Japanese economy would prevent potential Communist expansion to Japan and allow Japan to replace China as the economic hub of East Asia (Rotter 1987). The US military procurement from Japan for the Korean War and the Vietnam War further promoted the rise of Japan as a regional economic power. Other countries in Asia, such as Taiwan and South Korea, also benefited from American aid and US military expenditure during the Vietnam War to offset their chronic trade deficits. American policymakers saw that with the Japanese cooperation, they could shape the "technocratic states" (Taiwan and South Korea) in Asia. While the US delivered financial assistance and opened up its markets, Japan exported technology and carried out foreign direct investment (FDI) projects in Taiwan and South Korea (Halevi 1998). With a designed industrialization pattern in the region, specific trade relations among the US, Japan, Taiwan, South Korea, and other Asian countries developed: Japan and other Asian nations gained their trade surplus via exporting their goods to the US but most of the Asian countries had a trade deficit with Japan because of the large imports of Japanese high technology and capital goods. In short, without the US tolerance of imported goods from the Asian countries, it is hard to imagine how the "Asian economic miracle" could have been achieved.

These three factors mentioned above are equally essential in explaining Taiwan's and South Korea's post-war development. Alone they cannot explain for the two countries' economic achievement. For example, the entrepreneurial effort would not have succeeded without the favorable policy support. Similarly, the state policies would not operate well without the coordination of the international environment and domestic enterprises. Taiwan's and South Korea's economies would not have benefited from the favorable international economic environment without the other two factors. In other words, these three perspectives all have their advantages and insufficiencies. It would not be possible to interpret the development of Taiwan and South Korea without one of them. As such, some authors have tried to combine these different views. One of the combinations of the three is the *eclectic approach* taken by Koo H. (Koo 1987). From Koo's point of view, the interaction among the state, social class, and world system is more important than each individual variable in the development process. In his investigation of the cases of Taiwan and South Korea, the entrance of the two Asian tigers into the world system during the Cold War era was mostly due to political rather than economic reasons. He argued that without the support of the US and a relatively weak class force in the domestic societies, the states could not have become stronger. Clark's *comparative case study approach* suggested that Taiwan's success include "a possible unique combination of long-term structural and more short and idiosyncratic behavioral factors". The important structural conditions include the colonial legacy, Taiwan's dependency on the US, the availability of a profitable niche in the global economy, Taiwan's resource endowment, and the strong global demand for labor-intensive manufactured products. The important behavioral contributions include the state's heavy investment in "human capital", the success of land reform, the entrepreneurial skills and Taiwan's different ethnic groups (Clark 1987). Another example that takes a broader perspective on Taiwan's and South Korea's development is Cuming's approach of the *bureaucratic-authoritarian industrializing regime* (BAIR). The Japanese colonial foundation interacted with the imperatives of the Cold War to produce what he called the "BAIR". According to Cuming, the existence of the BAIR in both Taiwan and South Korea prevented the governments from being influenced by domestic interest groups. Weak society and strong state allowed both governments to have more flexibility to implement the policies favorable for economic development. He also argued that instead of investigating individual nations' economic progress, it is necessary to observe the industrial development in Taiwan, South Korea, and Japan as a whole because these economic developments are actually a "regional phenomenon". The American hegemonic system, in which the core state, semi-periphery, and periphery interact during the development process, is indispensable for functioning of the regional political economy (Cumings 1984).

AFC as a Watershed

The AFC has transformed Korea's economy into a neoliberal one, with more economic opening up. Taiwan, in response to the AFC, has tried to curb its overdependence on China's economy. Although South Korea suffered more from the AFC, it was able to bounce back more quickly than Taiwan a few years after the crisis. However, Taiwan's relatively well-developed economy in terms of GDP per capita, lower unemployment rate, and well-distributed income vis-à-vis South Korea is no longer the case after AFC. The diverse development between the two countries after the AFC is summarized as follows.

South Korea's Relatively More Resilient Economy

As shown in Fig. 1.2, South Korea's economy declined sharply to −5.5 percent in 1998 whereas Taiwan maintained a moderate expansion of 4.2 percent. Nonetheless, South Korea recovered from the AFC after only a year of the International Monetary Fund's (IMF) bailout, payment reprogramming, and a tight monetary policy. Although Taiwan's economy held up relatively well during the AFC, its economy progressed relatively more

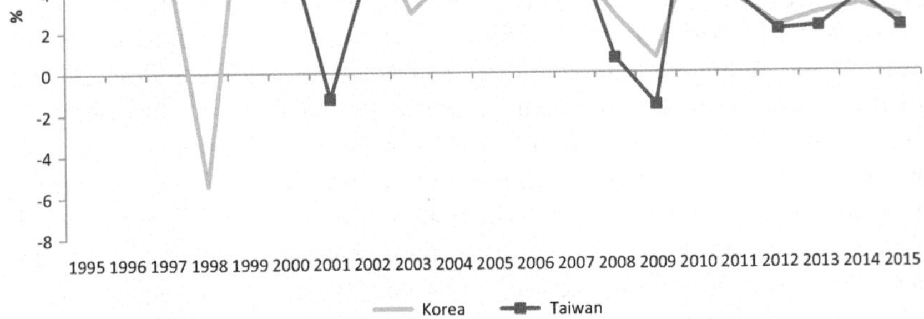

Fig. 1.2 Taiwan and South Korea's annual economic growth rates 1995–2016. Source: International Monetary Fund (2015)

slowly than that of South Korea after the crisis. The vulnerability of Taiwan's economy became even more apparent during the US internet bubble burst in the early 2000s and the global financial crisis (GFC) in 2008 and 2009. Its economic growth decreased to a historical low of −1.3 percent in 2001 and −1.6 percent in 2009. In contrast, South Korea's economy recorded a respective 5 percent and 0.7 percent of expansion. However, with the post-crisis rebound in 2011, both have suffered from the weak global demand and growing competition from Chinese manufacturers in the global market. Nevertheless, South Korea's economic growth after the GFC was still slightly higher than Taiwan's.

South Korea's GDP per Capita Has Surpassed Taiwan Since 2003

South Korea's greater economic expansion is also reflected in its more rapid development of GDP per capita. Taiwan had enjoyed higher GDP per capita than South Korea since the end of WWII. However, since 2003, it has been surpassed by South Korea and the gap has been enlarging especially after the GFC. In 2015, Taiwan's GDP per capita was US$22,082, clearly lower than South Korea's US$27,512 (Fig. 1.3). However, measured by purchasing power parity (PPP), Taiwan's GDP per capita (US$49,827) is much higher than South Korea's (US$39,387). Taiwan's low inflation rate and relatively lower living costs have made its GDP per capita at PPP relatively higher than South Korea's.

More Rapid Growth of Taiwan's Income Inequality Ratio

During the post-war industrialization period, Taiwan had enjoyed well-distributed income when the economy grew at high speed. Nevertheless, Taiwan's income gap has been worsening over the last decade. According to Cyrus Chu, a prestigious economist in Taiwan, the wage gap between the highest 5 percent and the lowest 5 percent of income groups had increased from 33 times in 1998 to 97 times by 2011. Figures from the World Fact book also showed that Taiwan's Gini index gradually enlarged from 32.6 in 2000 to 33.8 in 2012, indicating the growing income disparity. In comparison, South Korea's Gini index has clearly improved from 35.8 in 2000 to 30.2 by 2013 according to the World Fact book (Data source: Central Intelligence Agency).

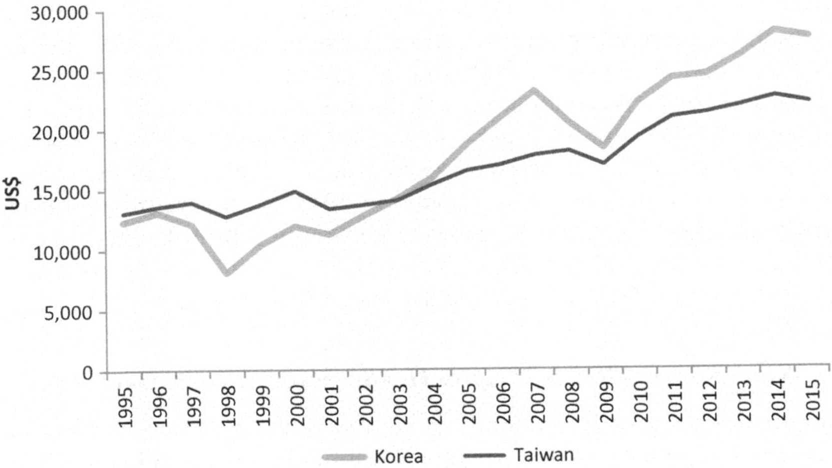

Fig. 1.3 Taiwan and South Korea's per capita GDP 1995–2015. Source: International Monetary Fund (2015)

South Korea Received More FDI than Taiwan

FDI is essential for developing countries to acquire technology and know-how from advanced countries. As such, many developing countries promoted FDI to attain economic development. Unlike Taiwan, the Korean government did not implement inward FDI promotion policy in its post-war industrialization. Hence, South Korea's foreign capital was mostly short-term foreign borrowing, making it vulnerable to the AFC. After the crisis, the government began to recognize the country's structural weakness and revised the policy to encourage FDI. As shown in Fig. 1.4, FDI in South Korea declined after 2000 but surged in 2004. FDI to South Korea has surged again since 2008. In comparison, FDI to Taiwan fell sharply after the GFC. Even with the policy promotion, Taiwan was not able to attract large amounts of FDI. According to the World Investment Report in 2015, Taiwan is one of the least attractive investment destinations in East Asia. Taiwan's attractiveness to foreign investors lags behind that of its regional peers, including not only South Korea but also Hong Kong and Singapore. The only East Asian countries with less FDI were Mongolia and North Korea, while of the ASEAN countries, only Brunei, Cambodia, Lao, and Myanmar were less appealing than Taiwan. Limited

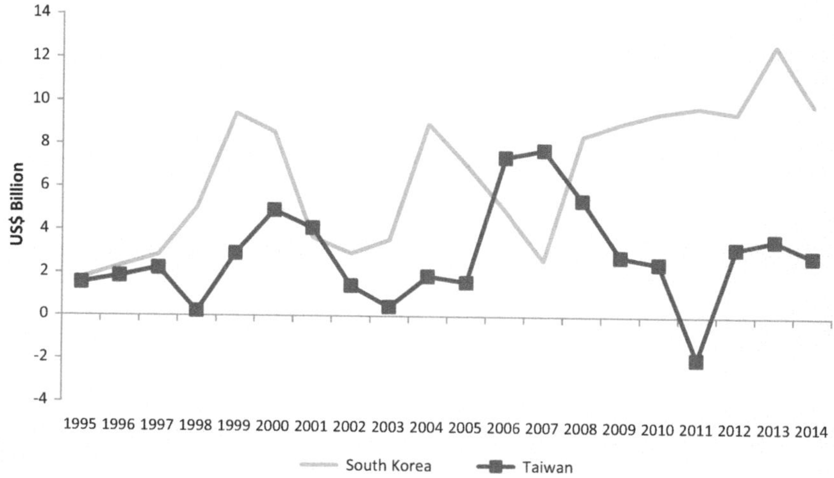

Fig. 1.4 Inward FDI in Taiwan and South Korea 1995–2014. Source: World Investment Report, UNCTD (various years)

market potential, a relatively high income tax, and inefficient judicial system are often considered as important reasons that deter foreign investors to Taiwan.

South Korea's Relatively Lower Unemployment Rate

One year after the AFC, a huge number of people in Korea suffered from layoffs and early retirement whereas the unemployment problem in Taiwan was relatively less serious. The unemployment rate in South Korea declined quickly from 6.3 percent in 1999 to 3.3 percent by 2002. Since 2002, South Korea's unemployment rate has maintained relatively stable, between 3.1 percent and 3.7 percent. On the contrary, Taiwan has suffered from a growing unemployment problem since 2001. Over the past 15 years (2000–2015), Taiwan's annual unemployment rate remained around 4–5 percent, slightly higher than that in South Korea (3–4 percent) (Fig. 1.5). Despite Taiwan's higher unemployment rate than before, it is still low compared to most of the Western countries. In fact, underlying the unemployment issue is the talent deficit problem. The number of Taiwanese people working in overseas countries increased from 0.34 million in 2005 to 0.72 million by 2015, according to Taiwan's Directorate

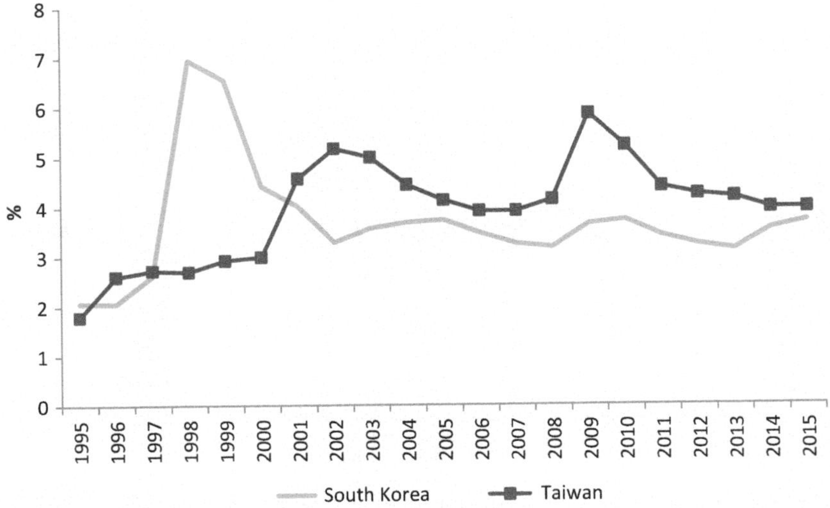

Fig. 1.5 Taiwan and South Korea's unemployment rate 1995–2015. Source: International Monetary Fund (2015)

General of Budget, Accounting and Statistics (DGBAS). Most of them are highly skilled workers. Oxford Economics' report indicated that Taiwan would have the most serious talent deficiency in 2021 among the 46 countries investigated whereas South Korea ranked the 40th (Oxford Economics 2012).

At the industry level, Korea's chaebols in the information and telecommunication technology (ICT) sector have successfully grasped a significant share in the global market over the last two decades. Today, Korea's ICT giants such as Samsung and LG are leading ICT branded products in the world. In comparison, Taiwan's economy continued to depend on OEM with low-profit margins. Although some Taiwanese brands have emerged in the downstream area, such as HTC, ACER, ASUS, BenQ, and D-Link, they are not able to seize important global market shares. Moreover, unlike Taiwan's dependence on ICT alone to sustain its economy, Korea's industry is more diversified. In recent years, Korean chaebols have expanded successfully into international markets from ICT and shipbuilding to entertainment, restaurants, and retail.

Research Questions, Objectives, Strategies, and Organization of the Book

Why did Taiwan's economy perform relatively well during the post-war development period but then progress at a more sluggish rate compared to that of South Korea over the last 20 years? Why was South Korea able to improve its overall economy after the AFC whereas Taiwan started to suffer from lower economic growth, higher unemployment rate, and growing income inequality? Can we find an answer for Taiwan's and South Korea's dissimilar development today from the conventional theories? If not, how can we explain the two countries' diverse development paths after the AFC? How can we construct a new model of post-industrial development based on the experiences of Taiwan and South Korea? What are the new lessons for developing countries from Taiwan's and South Korea's experiences?

To answer the above questions, we need to have a comprehensive understanding and detailed analysis of the macroeconomic figures. We need to explore the stories behind the statistics, such as the modification of government policy, alternations of international environment, and changes in domestic economic structure. We have set our research strategies and methods as follows. First, we suppose that the conventional explanations, including private sector effort, state policy, and foreign countries' influence, remain central in Taiwan's and South Korea's post-industrial development. Hence, we will examine Taiwan's and South Korea's development over the last two decades through these three perspectives. That means we will explore the new roles of private sector, government policy, and foreign influence in Taiwan's and South Korea's post-industrial economic development. How did SMEs and large companies contribute to the two countries' economic development in the last two decades? To what extent have certain economic policies been the engines of economic growth? How have foreign countries and the external environment impacted on the economic development of Taiwan and South Korea?

Next, the more specific timeframe is set from around the mid-1990s to the present. The reason for selecting this time period is that the post-war economic growth model based on exporting goods to the Western countries began to change around the mid-1990s. Both countries started to invest massively in developing countries, particularly in China, since the mid-1990s. The relocation of factories to overseas countries also implied that both economies no longer held comparative advantages in labor-intensive manufacturing production. This shows that the two countries had slowly moved away from the traditional growth model based on exporting manufactured goods to the Western countries. Both countries turned to rely on exporting intermediate goods to developing countries, mainly to China, for sustaining economic growth. At the same time, both countries continued to depend on importing capital goods and key components from Japan.

Third, macroeconomic figures from official statistics in both Taiwan and South Korea are extensively employed to evaluate both countries' development. The comprehensive use of statistics allows the book to present the main features of post-industrial development. It also helps to elucidate and compare the development stories in Taiwan and South Korea.

The remaining chapters in this book are structured as follows.

First of all, in contrast to the Cold War era when the US consolidated its partnership with Asian countries by opening up its market for Asian exports, China's economic reforms since the end of the 1970s have changed the political economy in the region. The "US factor" that affected Taiwan's and South Korea's economic development was therefore replaced by the "China factor". Relocating factories to China has become an important driver behind Taiwan's and South Korea's post-industrial development. Taiwan's and South Korea's growth patterns have changed from exporting final consumption goods to the US to exporting intermediate goods to China for final assembly. As such, in the second chapter, Taiwan's and South Korea's economic relations with China over the last two decades, including trade, investment, and their respective economic agreements, are examined. We will see how the economic engagement with China has supported Taiwan and Korea's economic development in the last two decades and consider the future prospects.

In the third chapter, private sector contribution to the economic development in Taiwan and South Korea over the last two decades is compared. We essentially compare SME development in both countries. SMEs were not only vital players in promoting Taiwan's export-oriented economic growth but also an important contributor in equalizing Taiwan's income equality. Unlike Taiwan, Korea's economy has been driven by chaebols. Nonetheless, the South Korean government noticed the importance of SMEs and began to promote SME development since the end of the 1980s. During the wave of globalization, Taiwan's large firms and Korea's chaebols seemed more able to expand their businesses abroad whereas

SMEs are more vulnerable to the global economic fluctuations. By comparing SME development in the two countries, this chapter also shows that the large corporation has prevailed in modern capitalist development in Taiwan and South Korea. This helps to provide a better understanding of the economic structural transformation of both countries during the post-industrial development period.

When recounting Taiwan's and South Korea's post-war development, the governments' intervention is often highlighted. Hence, in the fourth and the fifth chapters, we will examine whether the governments in Taiwan and South Korea still play an important role in their post-industrial development. During the post-war industrialization period, the governments in both Taiwan and South Korea mainly focused on export promotion and economic liberalization. In the face of China's economic rise and the trend of globalization, the policies foci are different now. We will essentially compare the effectiveness of industrial upgrading policies and the Free Trade Agreement (FTA) strategy adopted by the Taiwanese and Korean governments in dealing with the new challenges.

Development is a continuous process and it is not only about GDP growth. In recent years, more social concerns have emerged in both Taiwan and South Korea. Of particular interest is the growing income inequality. Several surveys showed that people in both countries are not satisfied with their current living conditions after experiencing successful post-war industrialization. However, the Gini index showed that the income inequality in Taiwan and South Korea is not as serious as that of other countries. This is not to say that the income inequality is not real or unimportant. The point is that there is a need to explore how and why people feel the growing income inequality. Another emerging social issue is that of aging population. As such, it is important to make sure that the production of goods and services are able to finance the welfare spending for the unemployed, elderly, and others in need of financial assistance. How such social issues have evolved and what the governments in Taiwan and South Korea have done so far to tackle these new challenges are addressed in the sixth and the seventh chapters.

The concluding chapter will bring together the main points raised in the previous chapters, reconsider and advance the conventional development theories through comparing these two empirical cases, and, in closing, provide an outlook for future development in both Taiwan and South Korea.

References

Adelman, I. (1999). State and market in the economic development of Korea and Taiwan. In T. Erik & H. Wan (Eds.), *Taiwan's development experience: Lessons on role of government and market* (pp. 289–326). Boston, MA: Kluwer Academic Publishers.

Berger, M. T. (2004). *The battle for Asia: From decolonization to globalization.* New York: Routledge Curzon.

Byun, H. Y. (1993). Economic development and inflation: Lessons from the Korean experience. *Journal of Asian Economics, 4*(2), 313–330.

Central Intelligence Agency. The World Fact book. Retrieved January 4, 2016., from https://www.cia.gov/library/publications/the-world-factbook/fields/2172.html

Chiang, M.-H. (2016). *China-Taiwan Rapprochement: The political economy of cross-strait relations.* London and New York: Routledge.

Clark, C. (1987). The Taiwan exception: Implication for contending political economy paradigm. *International Studies Quarterly, 31*(3), 327–356.

Cumings, B. (1984). The origins and development of the Northeast Asian political economy: Industrial sectors, product cycles, and political consequences. *International Organization, 38*(1), 1–40.

Evens, P., & Pang, C.-K. (1989). State structure and state policy: Implications of the Taiwanese case for newly industrializing countries. In H.-H. M. Hsiao, W.-Y. Cheng, & H.-S. Chan (Eds.), *Taiwan, a newly industrialized state* (pp. 3–22). Taipei: Pioneer Printing Co. Ltd.

Ha, Y.-C., & Lee, W. H. (2007). The politics of economic reform in South Korea: Crony capitalism after ten years. *Asian Survey, 47*(6), 894–914.

Haggard, S. (1990). *Pathways from the periphery: The politics of growth in the newly industrializing countries.* New York: Cornell University Press.

Halevi, J. (1998). The accumulation process in Japan and East Asia as compared with the role of Germany in European post-war growth. *Department of Economics, the University of Sydney, Working papers in Economics, 98*(04), 1–14.

Hattori, T., & Sato, Y. (1997). A comparative study of development mechanisms in Korea and Taiwan: Introductory analysis. *The Developing Economies, 34*(4), 341–357.

Hayashida, M. (1994). Entrepreneurship in Taiwan and Korea: A comparison. *Asia-Pacific Review, 1*(1), 59–82.

Ho, S. P. S. (1987). Economics, economic bureaucracy and Taiwan's economic development. *Pacific Affairs, 60*(2), 226–247.

Hu, M.-W., & Schive, C. (1998). The changing competitiveness of Taiwan's manufacturing SMEs. *Small Business Economics., 11*, 315–326.

Hundt, D. (2009). *Korea's developmental alliance: State, capital and the politics of rapid development.* London and New York: Routledge.

International Monetary Fund. (2015). World Economic Outlook Database. Retrieved March 8, 2016, from http://www.imf.org/external/pubs/ft/weo/2016/01/weodata/index.aspx

Kim, C. (1990). Labor market developments in macroeconomic perspective. In J. K. Kwon (Ed.), *Korea economic development* (pp. 303–321). Westport, CT: Greenwood.

Kim, K. S. (1991). The Korean miracle (1962–1980) revisited: Myths and realities in strategy and development. Working paper, No. 166, Kellogg Institute. Retrieved September 10, 2017, from https://kellogg.nd.edu/sites/default/files/old_files/documents/166_0.pdf

Koo, H. (1987). The interplay of state, social class, and world system in East Asia development: The cases of South Korea and Taiwan. In F. C. Deyo (Ed.), *The political economy of the new Asian industrialism* (pp. 165–181). Ithaca: Cornell University Press.

Kraemer, K. L., Linden, G., & Dedrick, J. (2011). Capturing value in global networks: Apple's iPad and iPhone. Retrieved June 27, 2017, from http://pcic.merage.uci.edu/papers/2011/value_ipad_iphone.pdf

Lee, Z.-R., & Hsiao, H.-H. M. (2014). Taiwan: SME-oriented capitalism in transition. In M. A. Witt & G. Redding (Eds.), *The Oxford handbook of Asian business system* (pp. 1–26). Oxford: Oxford University Press.

Li, K.-W. (2002). *Capitalist development and economism in East Asia: The rise of Hong Kong, Singapore, Taiwan and South Korea*. London and New York: Routledge.

Lim, W. (2003). The emergence of the chaebol and the origins of the chaebol problem. In S. Haggard, W. Lim, & E. Kim (Eds.), *Economic crisis and corporate restructuring in Korea* (pp. 35–54). Cambridge: Cambridge University Press.

Lin, Y. Y. (1998). Success factors of small and medium-sized enterprises in Taiwan: An analysis of cases. *Journal of Small Business Management, 36*(4), 43–59.

Minns, J. (2001). Of miracles and models: The rise and decline of the developmental state in South Korea. *Third World Quarterly, 22*(6), 1025–1034.

Oxford Economics. (2012). Global Talent 2021. Retrieved October 13, 2017, from http://www.oxfordeconomics.com/my-oxford/projects/128942

Rotter, A. J. (1987). *The path to Vietnam: Origins of the American commitment to Southeast Asia*. Ithaca: Cornell University Press.

Scitovsky, T. (1986). Economic development in Taiwan and South Korea, 1965–1981. In L. J. Lau (Ed.), *Models of development: A comparative study of economic growth in South Korea and Taiwan* (pp. 135–195). San Francisco, CA: Institute for Contemporary Studies.

Taniura, T. (1992). The industrialization of Taiwan: Introduction. In T. Taniura (Ed.), *Taiwan's industrialization: The formation of international processing base of operation* (pp. 1–16). Taipei: Ren-jen Publisher. (in Chinese).

Tsai, M.-C. (1999). Geopolitics, the state, and political economy of growth in Taiwan. *Review of Radical Political Economics, 31*(3), 101–109.

Wade, R. (1990). *Government and market: Economic theory and the role of government in East Asian industrialization.* Princeton, NJ: Princeton University Press.

World Investment Report. (n.d.) United Nations Conference on Trade and Development (various years).

Wu, Y. (2005). *A political explanation of economic growth: State survival, bureaucratic politics and private enterprises in the making of Taiwan's economy, 1950–1985.* Cambridge and London: Harvard University Asia Center.

Yoo, J. G. (1990). Income distribution in Korea. In J. K. Kwon (Ed.), *Korea economic development* (pp. 373–391). Westport, CT: Greenwood.

Yu, L.-L. T. (2009). Towards a structural model of a small family business in Taiwan. *Journal of Small Business and Entrepreneurship, 22*(4), 413–428.

CHAPTER 2

Sustaining Taiwan's and South Korea's Post-Industrial Economic Growth: The China Factor

Abstract Both Taiwan and South Korea shared similar investment evolution in China, including the investment from SMEs to large firms, from labor-intensive manufacturing to ICT sectors, and from regions close to the home countries to Shanghai and Jiangsu Province. In terms of trade relations, the greater exports to than import from China has allowed both countries to run a tremendous trade surplus vis-à-vis China. After China's industrial catchup in recent years, the growth model based on exporting intermediate goods to China is no longer workable. However, both Taiwan and South Korea have not yet found an alternative to completely replace the role of China. Both countries are facing unprecedented challenges to their economic growth prospects.

Keywords Foreign direct investment (FDI) in China • Taiwan-China trade relations • South Korea-China trade relations • Economic Cooperation Framework Agreement (ECFA) • South Korea-China free trade agreement (FTA)

Taiwan's and South Korea's post-war economic development based on exporting final goods to the global market (mostly the US) and importing key components from Japan underwent dramatic changes after China's economic opening up at the end of the 1970s. Indeed, when Taiwan and South Korea suffered from rising production costs domestically and trade

M.-H. Chiang, *Post-Industrial Development in East Asia*,
https://doi.org/10.1007/978-981-13-0274-9_2

protectionism from the Western countries in the 1980s, China's cheap labor force, geographic proximity, and exclusion from Western countries' trade protectionism offered new opportunities for Taiwanese and South Korean manufacturers. Investing in China also allowed Taiwan and South Korean companies to expand the economies of scale and maintain their products' international competitiveness. As both countries began to rely on exporting intermediate goods to their subsidiaries in China for final assembly, China replaced the US and became a new source of their economic growth. Nonetheless, the growth pattern based on exporting intermediate goods to China has suffered setbacks in recent years. As mentioned in the previous chapter, Taiwan and South Korea have experienced subdued economic growth after the post-crisis peak in 2010. Taiwan's economic growth continued to decline from 3.8 percent in 2011 to 0.8 percent in 2015, bouncing back only slightly to 1.5 percent in 2016. With large government spending, the growth rates have been maintained relatively well in South Korea, wavering between 2.6 percent and 3.7 percent during the 2011–2016 period. The weak demand from the global market provided a partial reason for Taiwan's and South Korea's economic slowdown in recent years. China's industrial catching up and its own structural changes toward a more consumption-based economy are more important factors. In the face of China's economic structural changes, both Taiwan's and South Korea's economies are at the critical juncture for transformation.

This chapter aims to compare Taiwan's and South Korea's economic relations with China over the last two decades. Through the comparison, this chapter presents Taiwan's and South Korea's economic ties with China and shows how this economic closeness has contributed to and subsequently challenged their economic development later on. The close economic ties began with Taiwan's and South Korea's large outward direct investment (ODI) in China. As such, the first section provides a comparison of both countries' ODI in China. The second section elaborates on Taiwan and South Korea's trade relations with China following the massive investment in manufacturing sectors. With China's industrial catchup, the trade pattern with China has evolved. The production networks between Taiwan and China and between South Korea and China have transformed from vertical to horizontal relations. The third section compares Taiwan's and South Korea's institutionalized economic relations with China. It demonstrates how Taiwan and South Korea have tried to secure their national interests in the face of China's growing economy and industrial upgrading. Finally, this chapter concludes with main points raised in the previous analysis.

Comparison of Taiwan's and South Korea's Investment in China

Comparison of China's Importance in Taiwan and Korea's ODI Profile

China had opened up its economy to FDI since the end of the 1970s. However, it was not until the 1990s that Taiwan and South Korean investment in China has expanded quickly and extensively. 2.1 shows Taiwan's and South Korea's investment amounts in China from their respective

Table 2.1 Taiwan and South Korea's official statistics about investments in China 1991–2016

	Taiwan's investment in China		*South Korea's investment in China*	
	Amounts (US$ million)	*As % of total Taiwan's ODI*	*Amounts (US$ million)*	*As % of total South Korea's ODI*
1991	174.2	9.5	43.1	3.3
1992	247.0	21.8	140.5	10.4
1993	3168.4	65.6	264.0	18.2
1994	962.2	37.3	640.6	27.1
1995	1092.7	44.6	847.3	26.2
1996	1229.2	36.2	951.8	20.9
1997	4334.3	60.0	784.4	20.1
1998	2034.6	38.2	686.0	14.3
1999	1252.8	27.7	350.4	10.3
2000	2607.1	33.9	763.9	14.5
2001	2784.1	38.8	659.4	12.3
2002	6723.1	66.6	1101.0	27.1
2003	7698.8	66.0	1828.7	38.3
2004	6940.7	67.2	2422.9	37.0
2005	6007.0	71.1	2860.6	39.3
2006	7642.3	63.9	3499.6	29.5
2007	9970.5	60.6	5439.5	24.0
2008	10,691.4	70.5	3858.9	16.1
2009	7142.6	70.4	2476.0	12.0
2010	14,617.9	83.8	3657.0	14.8
2011	14,376.6	79.5	3537.5	12.2
2012	12,792.1	61.2	4036.9	14.2
2013	9190.1	63.7	5007.4	16.8
2014	10,276.6	58.2	3133.0	11.7
2015	10,965.5	50.5	4316.2	10.7
2016	9670.7	44.4	3994.9	8.2

Source: CEIC (2017), Taiwan's Investment Commission (2017)

official statistics. Taiwan has recorded much greater investment in China than South Korea since 1991. Although the AFC was an investment dampener, causing Taiwan and South Korean investments to plummet in 1999, they rebounded quickly in the following years. Both countries have also shown a clear investment surge after 2002. China's accelerated market opening up after its accession to the World Trade Organization (WTO) in 2001 was an important reason. While Taiwan's investment in China continued to grow after the GFC (from US$7.1 billion in 2009 to US$14.6 billion in 2010 and US$14.4 billion in 2011), South Korean investment in China has been moving slowly. After the dip in 2009, South Korea's ODI in China ranged between US$3.1 billion and US$5 billion during the 2010–2016 period.

In terms of investment shares, China occupied a much greater importance in Taiwan's total ODI profile. This share increased from 33.9 in 2000 to 83.8 percent in 2010. However, China's share in Taiwan's total ODI was almost halved to 44.4 percent in 2016. In comparison, China accounted for a less significant share in South Korea's total ODI. China's shares in South Korea's total ODI increased from 14.5 percent in 2000 to its peak of 39.3 percent in 2005 but declined quickly to 8.2 percent in 2016.

In fact, Taiwan had set strict restrictions to deter large investment in China in the 1990s due to the uncertain political relations across the Strait. In 1993, the "Regulations Governing Investment and Technical Cooperation with Mainland China" offered a list of channels in which Taiwan's firms could invest indirectly in China. However, any direct investment was still prohibited. The "Southward Policy" was launched twice in the 1990s with an aim to divert Taiwan investors' interests from China to Southeast Asia. Despite the policy discouragement, Taiwan's investment in China continued to surge. The still large investment in China showed that the government's policy restraints were ineffective. After 2000, Taiwan's Mainland investment rules were gradually relaxed. The Chen Shui-Bian administration (2000–2008) adopted a more liberalized economic policy toward China so as to regulate the outward investment more effectively. The Ma Ying-jeou administration (2008–2016) lifted investment restrictions furthermore as it considered the deregulation as being important for Taiwan companies to better compete in the global market (Chiang 2016). However, the more relaxed rules did not foster greater investment in China. Taiwan's investment in China apparently declined during the second term of Ma's administration (2012–2016).

Unlike Taiwan, the South Korean government sought to deepen economic relations with China after bilateral diplomatic relations were established in 1992. After the establishment of Sino-Republic of Korea (ROK) diplomatic ties, the bilateral agreements on investors' protection, trade, and scientific technology cooperation were signed. In 1993 and 1994, the agreements on shipping, postal and communication cooperation, industrial cooperation, and custom cooperation were signed (Wang 1996). The relatively cordial relations between South Korea and China facilitated South Korean companies' investment in China. Indeed, South Korea in the 1990s had liberalized its overall ODI regulations more than before. On the one hand, the government considered that the support of business activities abroad would help to enhance the competitiveness of the domestic economy. On the other hand, South Korea's entry to the Organization for Economic Co-operation and Development (OECD) in 1996 also made the country subject to the organization's liberalization code. Beyond the investment in developing countries, South Korean firms also invested in developed countries to avoid trade barriers (Roger van Hoesel 1999). As such, unlike Taiwan's overwhelming investment in China, South Korea's ODI destinations were more diversified.

However, the statistics from the Chinese government tell a totally different story. Before 2003, Taiwan invested much more than South Korea did in China. Since 2003, South Korea's investment in China has started to surpass Taiwan. Korea's share in China's total inward FDI has also begun to exceed Taiwan's share since 2003 (Table 2.2). In 2017, South Korea made US$8527 million in China whereas Taiwan's investment was only US$4965 million. Although South Korea still accounted for a larger share in China's total FDI, both Taiwan and Korea's importance in China's total FDI have been declining over the last decade.

From SMEs in Labor-Intensive Industries to Large Companies in ICT Sectors

Manufacturing has been the main targeted sectors for both Taiwan and South Korean investors in China. From the mid-1990s to the early 2000s, around 90 percent of Taiwan's ODI in China centered on the manufacturing sectors. After the mid-2000s, the importance of manufacturing in Taiwan's ODI in China clearly declined. At the same time, the importance of the services sectors increased. In 2015, nearly 60 percent of Taiwan's investment in China was in manufacturing sectors, a decline from 91.4

Table 2.2 China's official statistics about Taiwan and South Korea's investments in China 1991–2016

	Taiwan's investment in China		*South Korea's investment in China*	
	Utilized amounts (US$ million)	*As % of total FDI in China*	*Utilized amounts (US$ million)*	*As % of total FDI in China*
1997	8020	7.6	5110	4.8
1998	7183	6.8	3871	3.7
1999	6124	6.5	3190	3.4
2000	5092	5.5	3288	3.6
2001	6778	6.3	4830	4.5
2002	9386	7.8	6508	5.4
2003	8947	6.5	10,954	8.0
2004	8414	5.7	16,368	11.2
2005	5625	3.6	13,138	8.3
2006	5152	3.3	9292	5.9
2007	4355	2.3	9692	5.1
2008	4860	1.9	8493	3.2
2009	4424	2.0	6695	3.0
2010	4757	1.8	6647	2.5
2011	5555	1.8	6362	2.1
2012	7375	2.5	7033	2.4
2013	5746	1.9	8028	2.6
2014	5630	1.8	11,616	3.7
2015	4147	1.2	11,139	3.3
2016	5346	1.6	13,104	3.9
2017	4965	1.5	8527	2.6

Source: CEIC (2017)

percent in 1995 (Table 2.3). During the same period, the services in Taiwan's investment shares jumped from merely 8.4 percent to 40 percent. In comparison, although South Korea's ODI in China also gradually shifted from manufacturing to services, the changes are relatively less dramatic. Manufacturing accounted for 79.3 percent of total South Korean investment in China in 2015, declining from 84.3 percent in 1995. During the same period, the services share increased from 15.1 percent to 20.6 percent. It is interesting to note that the relative importance of manufacturing for Taiwan (91.4 percent) was higher than South Korea (80.4 percent) in 1995. Twenty years later, the manufacturing shares for Taiwan (59.6 percent) declined more sharply than South Korea (79.3 percent). In terms of services sectors' investment, Taiwan's financial services have taken

Table 2.3 Taiwan and South Korea's investment in China by sector 1995–2015

	Taiwan					*South Korea*				
	1995	*2000*	*2005*	*2010*	*2015*	*1995*	*2000*	*2005*	*2010*	*2015*
Manufacturing	91.4	91.5	87.9	74.0	59.6	84.3	76.5	80.4	75.2	79.3
Services	8.4	8.3	11.9	24.9	40.0	15.1	23.3	18.8	24.4	20.6
Others	0.2	0.2	0.2	1.1	0.4	0.6	0.2	0.8	0.3	0.1

Source: Taiwan's Investment Commission, Taiwan; Kora Exim Bank

a significant share since 2011. For South Korea, activities in finance, insurance, wholesale and retail trade, and real estate have been its major investment in services in China over the last decade.

In the early 1990s, both Taiwanese and South Korean companies venturing into China were mostly SMEs engaging in labor-intensive manufacturing sectors, such as garments and textiles, food processing and footwear, and so on. After the late 1990s, the ICT sectors led by large companies became more important. That transformation of investment sectors was still motivated by cost considerations. According to China's official statistics, ICT sectors accounted for 12.5–20.6 percent of Taiwan's total manufacturing investment in China during 2002 and 2010. During the same period, South Korea's shares were between 17.4 percent and 35.3 percent (Ministry of Commerce of People's Republic of China 2011). The shift of main investment sectors from labor-intensive industries to ICT sectors could be explained by Taiwan's and South Korea's industrial structure changes. Both Taiwan and South Korea have concentrated on producing ICT goods since the 1990s and China was an ideal place for the final assembly of ICT goods. In other words, relocating factories to China helped to complement the ICT production in Taiwan and South Korea. The share of ICT production value in Taiwan's GDP increased from 7.7 percent in 1990 to 18.6 percent in 2015. During the same period, ICT share in total manufacturing production doubled from 16 percent to 38 percent (National Statistics, Taiwan 2017). In South Korea, the ICT sectors started to develop quickly during the 1990s. The government promoted the development of ICT sectors so as to overcome the negative impact from the GFC on the economy. The ICT shares in South Korea's GDP and total exports were 8 percent and 30 percent respectively in 2015 (Electronics and Telecommunications Research Institute 2016). In addition, China's policy changes in favor of FDI in ICT sectors might have promoted the investment into more technology and capital-intensive industries. Since the mid-1990s, several preferential measures were launched for FDI in high-technology sectors. Like FDI in other manufacturing sectors, FDI in ICT was also export-oriented. Although China's exports of ICT goods have increased, it continues to rely on importing intermediate goods from foreign countries, such as Taiwan and South Korea (Chiang 2016).

Both Taiwan and South Korean ICT firms benefited from investing in China. According to an OECD report, among the top 250 ICT firms in the world in 2009, there were 18 in Taiwan, behind Japan's 52 and America's 75. In terms of companies' revenues, the same report identified Taiwan as the third largest global producer of ICT products, after the US and Japan. In the same year, South Korea was ranked the fifth, after the above countries and Germany (OECD 2010). Taiwan and Korean ICT firms supplied intermediate goods to China for the final assembly. As a result, Taiwan and South Korean ICT companies' massive sales were largely driven by the rise of China as major exporter of ICT goods. For example, 25 percent of the group sales of Samsung, South Korea's conglomerate in ICT, came from China in 2011 (Kim 2012). The growing global demand for ICT goods boosted those ICT companies' sales furthermore. Being Apple's main subcontractor and component supplier, the roll out of new has bolstered the shipment of Taiwan's exports in ICT components to China. Taiwan's major ICT component suppliers to Apple (such as Taiwan Semiconductor Manufacturing Co., Hon Hai Precision Industry Co., Pegatron Corp., and Wistron Corp.) all reported revenue increases in 2017.

Since China's implementation of the Minimum Wage Regulations in 2004, Taiwan and South Korean investors have shifted their business strategy to leverage on the huge potential consumption market. The survey of Taiwan's Ministry of Economic Affairs (MOEA) in 2015 showed that market potential is the primary motivation for Taiwan entrepreneurs investing in China, followed by companies' business strategy and labor cost (Taiwan's Ministry of Economic Affairs 2015). A survey in South Korea also displayed similar result. The survey in 2010 showed that more than 50 percent of South Korean companies investing in China aimed to explore their domestic market (China Daily, 6 April 2012). In the face of China's policy shift from exports of manufactured goods to domestic demand, South Korean chaebols have adjusted their strategies in China from being a simple assembly location to becoming the second headquarters for Samsung, LG, or Hyundai, encompassing production, sales, and R&D capacities

(Zhan 2005). South Korea's other retail sector giant, Lotte Group, also announced plans to open more stores in China to take advantage of the expected booming market in China to offset a relatively sluggish South Korean economy (China Daily, 13 August 2011).

Shift of Investment Destinations

Since the 1980s, China's establishment of special economic zones (SEZs) in Fujian and Guangdong Province had successfully drawn investments from Taiwan. In addition to the lower labor cost, the proximity between southeast China and Taiwan as well as similar language and cultural background were attractive factors. Unlike Taiwan's investment concentration in the eastern coastal regions of China (Fujian and Guangdong) in the 1980s and early 1990s, the majority of South Korea's investment in China was in the northeast region (Heilongjiang, Jilan, and Liaoning) and Yellow Sea Rim (Beijing, Hebei, and Shandong). Similar to Taiwan investors, proximity was an important consideration for most South Korean manufacturers. Some ethnic Koreans moved to the northeast part of China several hundred years ago and they share a similar culture and language with the people in South Korea.

The economic development in other parts of China in the following decades has introduced further diversity into Taiwan's and South Korea's investment destinations. Taiwan entrepreneurs have shown particular preference for investing in Jiangsu Province. According to China's official statistics, Shanghai and Jiangsu Province combinedly accounted for 64 percent of Taiwan's total investment in China in 2012, increased from 33.8 percent in 2002 (Table 2.4). During the same period, the importance of Fujian and Guangdong Province has obviously decreased. In comparison, South Korea's investment share in Shanghai and Jiangsu Province also increased during the 2002–2012 period. During the same period, South Korean investment share in Beijing also grew significantly whereas the share in Shandong slid from 54 percent to 17.9 percent. As mentioned, Taiwan and South Korea's investment motivation had changed from taking advantage of low labor cost to exploring the huge Chinese market. The shift of investment locations is thus reflective of a change in investment strategy, moving from emphasis on a city's production cost to a city's market potential.

Following China's wage hike, some Taiwan and South Korean companies also considered relocating their factories in China's inland regions where the operational cost is lower. Some large Taiwan manufacturing

Table 2.4 Taiwan and South Korea's investment in China by location in 2002 and 2012

	Taiwan		*South Korea*	
	2002	*2012*	*2002*	*2012*
Southeast of China				
Shanghai	5.6	11.2	1.9	5.8
Jiangsu Province	28.2	52.8	13.1	23.2
Fujian Province	12.6	7.0	1.1	n/a
Guangdong Province	14.7	4.3	1.8	4.3
Zhejiang Province	7.3	3.5	3.2	2.3
North and northeast of China				
Beijing	0.5	n/a	1	23.0
Tianjin	0.9	n/a	5	3.1
Shandong Province	10.9	2.9	54.0	17.9
Liaoning Province	3.8	5.1	10	3.6
Jilin Province	n/a	n/a	1.3	1.5
Central China				
Shaanxi Province	n/a	n/a	n/a	12.1
Anhui Province	0.8	1.6	1.0	n/a
Hunan Province	2.3	4.3	0.2	n/a
Jiangxi Province	3.0	2.3	n/a	n/a
Other regions in China	9.4	5.0	6.4	3.0

Source: Ministry of Commerce, PRC (in Chinese)

firms, such as Foxconn, Acer, and Inventec, have moved some of their plants to Chengdu and Sichuan in order to maintain their profitability and sought to lower costs by operating R&D centers in China's coastal cities. Similarly, South Korea's Samsung decided to invest in the Xi'an High-tech Industrial Development Zone to produce nanometer chips, mainly for its smart phones and tablet PCs (Asia News Monitor, 11 April 2016). R&D in China's coastal regions plays a supplementary role in product improvement, especially product lines for the Chinese market.

Investment-Driven Trade Relations with China: A Changing Pattern

China did not account for a large share in Taiwan's external trade in the 1990s. As shown in Table 2.5, China accounted for less than 5 percent of Taiwan's total exports and imports from 1995 to 1999. This could be

Table 2.5 Taiwan and South Korea's trade relations with China 1995–2015

	Taiwan's trade with China		*South Korea's trade with China*	
	China in Taiwan's total exports	*China in Taiwan's total imports*	*China in South Korea's total exports*	*China in South Korea's total imports*
1995	0.3	3.0	7.0	5.5
1996	0.5	3.0	8.3	5.7
1997	0.5	3.4	9.4	6.9
1998	0.8	3.9	9.0	6.9
1999	2.1	4.1	9.5	7.4
2000	2.9	4.4	10.7	8.0
2001	3.9	5.5	12.1	9.4
2002	7.8	7.0	14.6	11.4
2003	15.2	8.6	18.1	12.3
2004	19.9	10.0	19.6	13.2
2005	22.0	11.0	21.8	14.8
2006	23.1	12.2	21.3	15.7
2007	25.3	12.8	22.1	17.7
2008	26.2	13.1	21.7	17.7
2009	26.6	14.0	23.9	16.8
2010	28.0	14.3	25.1	16.8
2011	27.2	15.5	24.2	16.5
2012	26.8	15.1	24.5	15.5
2013	26.8	15.8	26.1	16.1
2014	26.2	17.5	25.4	17.1
2015	25.4	19.4	26.0	20.7

Source: CEIC (2017), World Trade Atlas (2017), Taiwan's Council for Economic Planning and Development (2015)

explained by the restrictions on commercial exchanges across the Strait. Most of the goods transported between Taiwan and China went through Hong Kong. As such, while China's share in Taiwan's total trade was small, Hong Kong's share in Taiwan's external trade was quite large. Before 2002, Taiwan's total trading amounts with Hong Kong were still larger than its trade with China. However, 33–43 percent of Taiwan's trade with Hong Kong was actually destined for China (Mainland Affairs Council 2017). With the progressive economic deregulation across the Strait however, Taiwan-Hong Kong economic relations have become less important for Taiwan.[1] Instead, China has taken an increasing share in Taiwan's external trade. The closer trade ties were developed with Taiwan's greater exports to then imports from China. However, a reversal in development has occurred in recent years. China's share in Taiwan's total exports remained relatively the same, between 25 percent and 28 percent during the 2007–2015 period. On the other hand, the importance of China in Taiwan's imports saw clear growth from 13.1 percent in 2008 to 19.4 percent in 2015.

China accounted for larger shares in South Korea's external trade than its shares in Taiwan's external trade during the 1990s. In recent years, the changes in Taiwan-China trade relations can also be found in South Korea-China trade. China's share in South Korea's exports has remained quite constant, around 24 percent to 26 percent during 2009 and 2015. However, China's share in South Korea's total imports progressed from 16.8 percent in 2009 to 20.7 percent in 2015 (Table 2.5).

The changes in the trade shares (stagnant exports to and greater imports from China) indicated that the nature of production relations has been moving from vertical to horizontal connection. This change in production network can be observed from the trade items. In 2015, electrical machinery was Taiwan and South Korea's most important export items to China, followed by optical and medical instruments. Among the products categorized in electrical machinery, both countries exported mostly electronic integrated circuits (a key component in making ICT goods) to China. At the same time, both countries imported electronic integrated circuits and final ICT goods (such as smartphones, tablets, computers) from China (Table 2.6). The considerable imports of electronic integrated circuits are an indication of China's growing importance as a main semi-industrial goods supplier in Taiwan and South Korea's manufacturing production. At the same time, the still large quantities of final ICT goods imported suggest that China remains an important final goods producer of ICT products.

[1] After the initiation of "three mini links" in 2001, free sea transportation, merchandise trade, and personnel exchanges between Taiwan's two offshore islands (Kinmen and Matsu) and two cities in Fujian province of China (Xiamen and Fuzhou) have led to an upswing in Taiwan's trade with China, surpassing its trade with Hong Kong since 2002. The three links in direct postal, trade, and transportation across the Strait have been fully implemented since 2008. Taiwan opened eight airports and three harbors to cater to direct trade and personnel traveling between the two sides.

Table 2.6 Taiwan and South Korea's main trading items with China in 2015

	Taiwan	*South Korea*
Main export items to China	Electrical machinery (37.4%) Optical and medical instruments (15.6%) Plastic (9.8%)	Electrical machinery (38.4%) Optical and medical instruments (14.4%) Machinery (11.0%)
Main import items from China	Electrical machinery (41.0%) Machinery (13.3%) Iron and steel (4.8%)	Electrical machinery (35.1%) Machinery (11.3%) Iron and steel (7.6%)

Note: The numbers in brackets indicate the shares in total Taiwan and South Korea's imports and exports
Source: World Trade Atlas (2017)

Taiwanese and South Korean companies' greater use of local procurement in China is a reason for the relatively less significant expansion of Taiwan and South Korea's exports to China. In 2012, 62 percent of China-based Taiwan firms in electronic parts and components manufacturing and computers and 66 percent of Taiwan companies in electronic and optical products manufacturing procured capital equipment locally in China; 57 percent and 49 percent of these two sectors procured raw materials in China in the same year. This is in sharp contrast to the year 2002, when the same survey showed that only 19 percent of Taiwan's electronic and electric equipment manufacturers in China procured capital equipment and intermediate goods from local firms in China (Chiang 2016). Similarly, in 2004, the share of components and semi-finished goods imported from South Korea among their subsidiaries in China was 46.5 percent but this ratio declined to 19.2 percent in 2010. During the same period, China-based South Korean firms' local procurement ratio increased from 38.6 percent to 64.7 percent (Chiang 2017).

South Korea has registered trade surplus with China since the 1990s while Taiwan started to have trade surplus with China since the early 2000s. Again, the restrictions on cross-strait commercial exchanges have biased the trade statistics between Taiwan and China. South Korea's trade surplus with China reached a new high in 2009 after the sharp fall in 2008. However, since 2013, both Taiwan's and South Korea's trade surplus with China have declined visibly. The stagnant exports to and greater imports from China have resulted in the shrinkage of Taiwan's and South Korea's trade surplus in recent years. As shown in Fig. 2.1, Taiwan's trade surplus with China reached the highest level in 2010 but has gradually been on

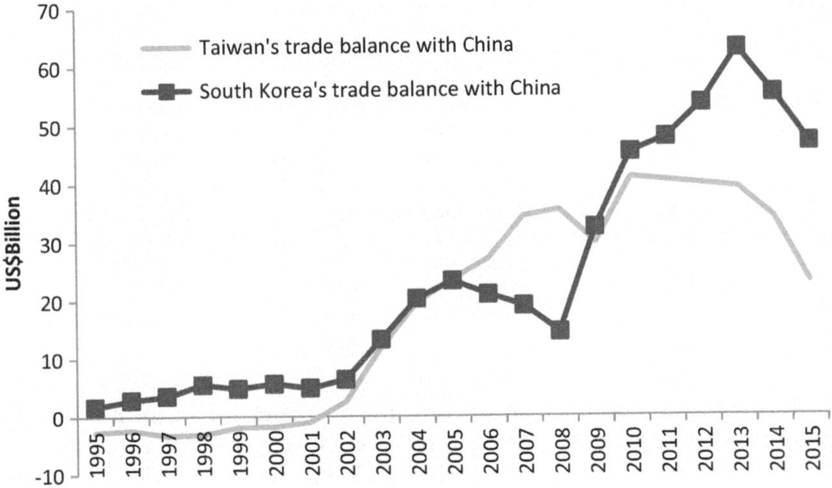

Fig. 2.1 Taiwan and South Korea's trade balance with China 1995–2015. Source: CEIC, World Trade Atlas, Taiwan Statistical Data Book 2015

the decline ever since. In 2015, Taiwan's trade surplus with China registered the largest decline to US$23 billion, from US$34.1 billion in the previous year. South Korea's trade surplus with China peaked in 2013 and has been declining since 2014. Net exports (exports minus imports) have been an important source of economic growth for both Taiwan and South Korea. As China is the largest trading partner of Taiwan and South Korea, the slowing of trade surplus has profound impact on both countries' economic growth.

Taiwan and South Korea's Institutional Responses: Comparison of the ECFA and South Korea-China FTA

Taiwan-China Economic Cooperation Framework Agreement

A historical Economic Cooperation Framework Agreement (ECFA) was signed between the Strait Exchange Foundation (SEF, on behalf of Taiwan) and Association for Relations across the Taiwan Straits (ARATS, on behalf of China) on 29 June 2010. The Ma administration expected the ECFA to boost Taiwan's economic growth. With a population of just over 1.3 billion, China's domestic market was not only huge but also rapidly growing. Many foreign investors found it difficult to enter. The Ma administration considered that Taiwan, with its similar linguistic and cultural background, its closer and legalized economic relationship with China, was likely to capture the attention of foreign investors who would want to cooperate with Taiwan entrepreneurs. The Ma administration also considered the ECFA as encouragement of other countries to sign free trade agreements (FTAs) with Taiwan; Taiwan has been excluded from the growing bilateral and multilateral FTAs trend over the last few decades. Ma's administration believed that Taiwan's minimal involvement in the FTAs would cast a shadow on the island's economic prospect, especially when the FTA between China and ASEAN took effect on 1 January 2011. ASEAN's trade negotiations with China, Japan, and South Korea to form ASEAN+3 were also believed by the government to further diminish Taiwan's economic significance in the region. The threat of marginalization in the region pushed Taiwan's government to pursue an economic agreement with China, Taiwan's largest trade partner.

The ECFA sets a basic framework for the subsequent free trade negotiations between Taiwan and China. The early harvest program under the ECFA covers those aspects of trade in goods and services that had been opened up first since 2011. With the early harvest program, China had to lower tariffs on 521 manufactured products and Taiwan has been doing the same for 267 items since January 2011. The tariffs of these items were reduced to zero in 2013. In terms of trade in services, China opened up 11 service sectors for Taiwanese investments while Taiwan opened 9 sectors (Table 2.7). After the early harvest program, the Cross-Strait Bilateral Investment Protection and Promotion Agreement took effect on 1 February 2013. However, the impact on Taiwan's economy from the ECFA has been limited because the products listed on the early harvest program accounted for a small portion of goods traded between Taiwan

Table 2.7 Brief summary of early harvest program of ECFA

	China opens to Taiwan	*Taiwan opens to China*
Agricultural products	18	0
Manufactured products	521	267
Services sector	11	9

Source: Taiwan's Ministry of Economic Affairs (2015)

and China (Chiang 2016). For example, in 2009, goods listed on the early harvest program accounted for 14 percent of Taiwan's total imports from China and 11 percent of China's total imports from Taiwan. In fact, the ECFA only provided a basic structure for the follow-up negotiations on overall trade in goods and services, namely the Cross-Strait Trade in Goods Agreement (CSTGA) and the Cross-Strait Service Trade Agreement (CSSTA). The implementation of CSSTA and CSTGA would have more significant impact on Taiwan's economy.

On 21 June 2013, the CSSTA was officially signed. Nonetheless, a coalition of students and civic groups launched the 24-day-long students' occupation of Taiwan's parliament (Sunflower Student Movement) on 18 March 2014 to stall the passage of the CSSTA in Taiwan's parliament. Student protestors believed that the pact was negotiated in secret, giving China greater political control of the island. They demanded for the implementation of an oversight mechanism to review the CSSTA. Indeed, the CSSTA is a much more complicated agreement than the CSGTA as it will permit service providers to work on the other side of the Strait. On the contrary, CSGTA will only allow free flow of goods between the two sides. The free flow of people is a particularly sensitive issue when Taiwan still regards China as a potential invader of the island. Hence, proceeding with the CSSTA (the more complicated one) before CSGTA (the easier one) shows the insensitivity of the government's cross-strait economic opening up strategy. The cross-strait supervisory rule was expected to provide a "safety net" for the government in its agreements with China. However, the dispute concerning the formulation of a supervisory rule has made the ratification of CSSTA a distant reality.

South Korea-China FTA

The South Korea-China FTA was signed on 1 June 2015 in Seoul after 14 rounds of negotiations since 2013. It incorporates 22 chapters and 7 annexes in total, covering not only trade in goods, trade in services and investment but also a variety of regulatory frameworks (e.g., competition policy, intellectual property rights, dispute settlement, e-commerce, transparency) for investment facilitation and further economic cooperation between the two countries.

Under the FTA, South Korea will completely eliminate its tariffs on 79 percent of all products imported from China within ten years (77 percent of imports amounts). On its part, China will remove tariffs on 71 percent of the products from South Korea over the same period (66 percent of import amounts). In 20 years, China and South Korea will eliminate tariffs on 92 percent and 93 percent of trade items respectively (Table 2.8). There are several features in this bilateral FTA.

First, China allows a limited tariff reduction for Chinese agricultural products on the part of South Korea in exchange for Chinese manufacturing goods' greater access to the South Korean market. In 20 years, only 70 percent of Chinese agricultural goods will enjoy zero tariffs compared to 93 percent set by China for South Korean agricultural goods. However, South Korea agrees to open up relatively more for manufacturing imports (97 percent of import items) than China does (90 percent).

Second, the slow path of opening up (in 20 years) indicates that the benefits for both countries from the deal could be insignificant in the short term. For example, LCDs made in South Korea are expected to benefit from tariff cuts in ten years after the FTA goes into effect. However, as

Table 2.8 Planned tariff reduction to zero between China and South Korea

	China's scheduled tariff reduction		*South Korea's scheduled tariff reduction*	
	Product items	*Import amounts*	*Product items*	*Import amounts*
1. General items				
In 10 years				
Manufacturing products	72%	66%	90%	80%
Overall products	**71%**	**66%**	**79%**	**77%**
2. Sensitive items				
In 20 years				
Agricultural products	93%	56%	70%	40%
Manufacturing products	90%	85%	97%	94%
Overall products	**92%**	**91%**	**93%**	**95%**
3. Super-sensitive items				
Excluded from concessions	Autos, paraxylene, terephthalic acid, etc.		Rice, chili, garlic, Chinese cabbage, apples, fisheries, livestock products, etc.	

Source: Contemporary South Korean economy: challenges and prospects, Chiang Min-Hua, Copyright 2017, World Scientific, Singapore

Chinese LCD makers are quickly catching up, the tariff reduction in a decade could be meaningless for South Korean LCD makers to capture China's market. From a positive point of view, this would help reduce potentially huge damages to farmers and industries from the two countries. Despite the slow implementation of tariff reduction, the economic cooperation measures in the FTA are expected to provide both sides with opportunities to further explore their business potential.

Third, the advantages and potential impact on bilateral manufacturing trade could be limited as a variety of manufacturing goods already enjoy zero tariffs. For example, ICT products accounted for the largest share in the bilateral trade relations. As members of the Information Technology Agreement (ITA) under WTO, both China and South Korea have already removed their tariffs on a variety of ICT goods. China exports many steel products to South Korea. Nonetheless, the FTA might not stimulate large exports of Chinese steel products because most steel products since 2004 under WTO rules have been set at zero tariffs (Business Korea, 11 November 2014a).

Fourth, the scope of tariff reduction is limited. Petrochemical products are one of South Korea's main export items. Except for hydrocarbons which will be set to zero tariffs under the FTA, other petrochemical products such as paraxylene, terephthalic acid, and ethylene glycol have been excluded from tariff concession (Business Korea, 11 November 2014a). China also excluded passenger cars from the negotiating table to protect its own automobile industry. However, the exclusion of automobiles[2] will not impact on South Korean car makers as they now sell their locally produced cars in China without the need to export from South Korea.

Fifth, a total of 310 products manufactured in the Kaesong Industrial Complex (located in North Korea and run by South Korea) would be subject to preferential tariffs right after the FTA implementation. This is expected to allow more benefits for the inter-Korean industrial park than any other free trade pacts that South Korea has signed so far.

Indeed, South Korea regards the traditional production network of supplying intermediate goods to China for final assembly as unsustainable in the long run. Hence, the bilateral FTA serves as a new channel for

[2] Passenger cars were excluded from the negotiation table. However, South Korea will abolish tariffs on gasoline buses and trucks from China within 15 years of the implementation, while China will eliminate duties on buses and trucks from South Korea within 20 years (Xinhua News Agency, 12 March 2015).

exporting consumer goods to the potentially huge market in China. For China, this is the first time that it includes "telecommunication" and "financial services" as separate chapters in its FTAs. China regards this as an initial step toward "high standard" FTAs with advanced countries in the future (Ministry of Commerce of People's Republic of China, 2 June 2015). The inclusion of environment, electronic commerce, and investment measures in the South Korea-China FTA is also considered as China's advancement in terms of FTA quality.

Moreover, both countries have agreed to open a variety of service sectors for mutual investment, covering several subsectors in business services, communication, construction, distribution, education, environment, financial services, tourism, recreational, cultural and sporting services, and transport services (Table 2.9). The main features of commitments in service sectors are summarized as follows.

Table 2.9 Specific commitments in services under China-ROK FTA

Sectors and subsectors	*China opens to South Korea's investment*	*South Korea opens to China's investment*
1. Business services		
1.1 Professional services	V	V
1.2 Computer and related services	V	V
1.3 Research and development services		V
1.4 Real estate services	V	V
1.5 Rental/leasing services without operators		V
1.6 Other business services	V	V
2. Communication services		
2.1 Courier services	V	V
2.2 Telecommunication services		V
2.3 Value-added services	V	V
2.4 Audiovisual services	V	V
3. Construction services	**V**	**V**
4. Distribution services		
4.1 Commission agents' services	V	V
4.2 Wholesale trade services	V	V
4.3 Retailing services	V	V
4.4 Franchising services	V	V

(*continued*)

Table 2.9 (continued)

Sectors and subsectors	*China opens to South Korea's investment*	*South Korea opens to China's investment*
5. Educational services		
5.1 Primary education services	V	
5.2 Secondary education services	V	
5.3 Higher education services	V	V
5.4 Adult education services	V	V
5.5 Other education services	V	
6. Environmental services		
6.1 Sewage services	V	V
6.2 Refuse disposal services	V	V
6.3 Clearing of exhaust gases services	V	
6.4 Noise abatement services	V	
6.5 Sanitation services	V	
6.6 Natural and landscape protection services	V	
6.7 Other environmental protection services	V	
7. Financial services		
7.1 Insurance and insurance related services	V	V
7.2 Banking and other financial services	V	V
8. Tourism and travel services		
8.1 Hotel and restaurants	V	V
8.2 Travel agencies and tour operators services	V	V
8.3 Tourist guides services		V
9. Recreational, cultural, and sporting services		
9.1 Entertainment services	V	V
9.2 Sporting and other recreational services	V	
10. Transport services		
10.1 Maritime transport services	V	V
10.2 Air transport services	V	V
10.3 Retail transport services	V	V
10.4 Road transport services	V	V
10.5 Pipeline transport		V
10.6 Services auxiliary to all modes of transport	V	V
10.7 Other transport services		V

Source: Contemporary South Korean economy: challenges and prospects, Chiang Min-Hua, Copyright 2017, World Scientific, Singapore

First, China has advanced opening measures for South Korea in legal services, construction, environment and recreational, cultural and sporting services while South Korea's opening for China's investment in courier services and construction is superior to its commitments to other countries so far. Chinese companies in courier services and construction can begin operations in South Korea without setting up representative offices (China Daily, 3 June 2015).

Second, the IPR measure is expected to boost the South Korean entertainment industry as South Korean companies can have up to 49 percent stake in Chinese entertainment firms. China is an important market for South Korean drama makers (Business Korea, 26 December 2014b). More joint production in cinema, TV dramas, and broadcasting between the two countries is expected.

Third, the bilateral FTA would also encourage investment in financial sectors and telecommunications between the two countries. Although Koreans are concerned about the potential large presence of Chinese telecommunication business in South Korea, the prospects of their financial institutions benefiting from greater access to China's financial market through the FTA could be more than sufficient to offset the setback (Business Korea, 11 November 2014a).

Fourth, following the potential large investment between the two countries, the facilitation of people's movement from the two sides is important. China and South Korea agree to allow their citizens to apply for multiple entry visas provided that there is no criminal record on their first visit. For internal dispatch in the same company, both South Korean citizens and foreigners can enjoy two years of long-term residency in China. The same special treatment is applied to the Chinese in South Korea (Ministry of Commerce, 2 June 2015).

Beyond the service sectors, China is interested in South Korea's high-end manufacturing industries for their more advanced technologies. The "made in Korea" brand reputation and South Korea's wider FTA network with both developing and developed countries are also attractive to Chinese investors.

Conclusion

This chapter compares Taiwan's and South Korea's economic relations with China in terms of trade, investment, and institutionalized economic agreements. The main findings from the previous analysis are summarized as follows. First, Taiwan's investment in China has been much larger than South Korea's investment according to Taiwan and South Korea's official statistics. Taiwan's greater investment amounts suggest its investment policy constraints toward China were ineffective. On the contrary, the South Korean government did not enact particular investment restrictions toward China. Taiwan's much larger ODI in China (in terms of its total ODI shares and absolute amounts) also showed that Taiwanese entrepreneurs overwhelmingly relied on China to maintain their profitability whereas South Korean manufacturers had a more diversified investment strategy. However, China's official statistics showed that Korean investment in China was much greater than Taiwan after 2003. Despite the differences in investment amounts, both countries show a similar investment pattern. Both had been attracted by China's low labor costs and geographical proximity in the beginning and later by China's huge consumption market. The investments were initially led by SMEs in labor-intensive manufacturing sectors and then by large companies in ICT sectors. Taiwan entrepreneurs initially relocated factories to cities in China's east coastal regions. South Korean firms invested mostly in the northeast of China at the initial stage. With China's greater economic opening up, both have since shifted their investment locations to Shanghai and Jiangsu Provinces.

Second, Taiwan's and South Korea's investment in China has been the main driver behind their growing exports to the country. Despite South Korea's more diversified investment destinations compared to Taiwan, both have depended on exporting intermediate goods to China for their economic growth. China's shares in both countries' exports and imports have been similar since 2004. The reason for China's relatively lower shares in Taiwan's trade in the 1990s and the early 2000s could be the trade restrictions across the Taiwan Strait. Both Taiwan and South Korea have encountered changes in bilateral trade with China in recent years. While Taiwan's and South Korea's exports to China have remained significant, their imports from China have also become important. As such, both countries' trade surpluses with China have been declining. With China's industrial catchup and wage hike, the country is no longer a suitable place for assembling final goods for Taiwan and South Korean manufacturers. Instead, some Chinese manufacturers are now in direct competition with Taiwanese and South Korean companies. This signifies that the growth models based on exporting intermediate goods to China are ending. Despite China's vast and growing market potential, it has not formed an effective demand for Taiwanese and South Korean goods. Taiwan and South Korea's slower economic growth in recent years indicates that a new growth model has yet to be found.

Third, both countries have tried to secure their economic interests through the establishment of institutionalized economic relations with China. The ECFA set up a framework for follow-up trade and investment negotiations between Taiwan and China. Nevertheless, political concerns have blocked the passage of the CSSTA in Taiwan's parliament. China has refused to talk with Taiwan's Democratic Progressive Party (DPP) administration since 2016. Unlike Taiwan's, South Korea's FTA with China has been proceeding relatively smoothly. The South Korea-China FTA is more comprehensive than the ECFA. However, the effect could be limited due to the slow path of full implementation and limited scope of tariff reductions. Indeed, South Korea and China have sought to expand economic cooperation beyond traditional processing trade through this FTA. South Korea expects to gain greater access to the Chinese market for Korean consumer goods and service business with China's push for a consumption-based economy. The follow-up negotiation on investment and services may promote greater economic opening up between the two countries.

Overall, Taiwan's and South Korea's investment in China created a new life line for sustaining both countries' economic growth when they faced worsening investment environments at home and trade protectionism from the Western countries. The success of China's export-led economic development can be interpreted as success of the production network established by Taiwanese and South Korean companies. However, the decline of the "world's factory" has made the growth model based on exporting to China no longer workable. Taiwan and South Korean firms have shifted labor-intensive manufacturing sectors to Southeast Asian countries, retaining only some high-value-added production and services in China. It remains to be seen how Taiwan and South Korea can find another source of economic growth through their new production ties with China and Southeast Asia.

References

Asia News Monitor. (2016, April 11). China: Samsung to build memory chip plant in Xi'an. Retrieved February 28, 2018, from http://libproxy1.nus.edu.sg/login?url=https://search.proquest.com/docview/993159

Business Korea. (2014a, November 11). Korea-China FTA opening new chapter of bilateral economic ties. Retrieved April 13, 2017, from http://www.businesskorea.co.kr/english/news/politics/7234-new-economic-ally-korea-china-fta-opening-new-chapter-bilateral-economic-ties

Business Korea. (2014b, December 26). Culture trade balance: Cultural exports to surpass 1 trillion won this year. Retrieved July 15, 2015, from http://www.businesskorea.co.kr/article/8231/culture-trade-balance-cultural-exports-surpass-1-trillion-won-year

CEIC Global Database. (2017). Retrieved September 28, 2017, from https://www.ceicdata.com/zh-hans

Chiang, M.-H. (2016). *China-Taiwan Rapprochement: The political economy of cross-strait relations.* London and New York: Routledge.

Chiang, M.-H. (2017). *Contemporary South Korean economy: Challenges and prospects.* Singapore: World Scientific.

China Daily. (2011, August 13). Lotte signals expansion in Chinese market. Retrieved April 17, 2013, from http://www.chinadaily.com.cn/business/2011-08/13/content_13105451.htm

China Daily. (2012, April 6). China-S. Korea pact first on agenda. Retrieved May 15, 2013, from http://www.chinadaily.com.cn/world/2012-04/06/content_14986771.html

China Daily. (2015, June 3). Ministry of commerce: China-ROK FTA will increase China's GDP by 0.34%. Retrieved July 15, 2015, from http://www.chinadaily.com.cn/micro-reading/china/2015-06-03/content_13788654.html

Council for Economic Planning and Development (Taiwan). (2015). *Taiwan statistical data book 2015.* Executive Yuan: Taipei.

Electronics and Telecommunications Research Institute. (2016). Korea IT strategy and ETRI. Retrieved September 18, 2017, from https://gcc.kaist.ac.kr/_prog/_board/common/download.php?code=comm_0303_kr&ntt_no=125&atch_no=6

Investment Commission (Taiwan). (2017). Monthly statistics. Accessed April 12, 2017, from http://www.moeaic.gov.tw/english/index.jsp

Kim, Dong-ha. (2012). Samsung finds a future in China. *POSRI Chindia Quarterly.* Retrieved April 12, 2017, from https://www.posri.re.kr/eng/board/section_content/2958

Mainland Affairs Council (Taiwan). (2017). Cross-strait monthly economic statistics (liang an jing ji tong ji yue bao). Retrieved February 28, 2018, from https://www.mac.gov.tw/News.aspx?n=2C28D363038C300F&sms=231F60B3498BBB19

Ministry of Commerce of People's Republic of China. (2011). *China Foreign Investment Report 2011(2011 zhong guo wai shang tou zi bao gao).* Beijing: Economy and Management Publishing House.

Ministry of Commerce of People's Republic of China. (2015, June 2). 50 inquiries about China-ROK FTA (zhong hua ren min gong he guo zheng fu he da han min guo zheng fu zi you mao yi xie ding 50wen). Retrieved June 10, 2015, from http://fta.mofcom.gov.cn/article/ftanews/201506/21871_1.html

Ministry of Economic Affairs (Taiwan). (2015). *What is the content in the early harvest program? When will it take effect? (zao shou qing dan nei rong wei he? he shi sheng xiao?)* Retrieved February 28, 2018, from http://www.ecfa.org.tw/ShowFAQ.aspx?id=70

National Statistics (Taiwan). (2017). Retrieved April 12, 2017, from http://www.stat.gov.tw/mp.asp?mp=4

Organisation for Economic Co-operation and Development (OECD). (2010). *OECD Information Technology Outlook 2010*. Paris: OECD Publishing.

Van Hoesel, R. (1999). *New multinational enterprises from Korea and Taiwan: Beyond export-led growth*. London and New York: Routledge.

Wang, Z. (1996). *Korean investment in China (Han guo qi ye zai zhong guo de tou zi)*. Beijing: China Economic Publishing House.

World Trade Atlas. (2017). Global Trade Information Services, Inc. Retrieved September 28, 2017, from http://www.gtis.com/wta.htm

Xinhua News Agency. (2015, March 12). Hyundai to boost localization after China-S.Korea FTA. Retrieved February 28, 2018, from http://www.china.org.cn/world/Off_the_Wire/2015-03/12/content_35030787.htm

Zhan, X. (2005, January/February). *Analysis of South Korea's investmentin China*. China & World Economy.

CHAPTER 3

The Changing Role of SMEs in Taiwan's and South Korea's Economies

Abstract In the last two decades, large companies have made greater contribution to Taiwan and South Korea's export-oriented economic growth whereas SMEs' importance has been declining. This is especially a big contrast in Taiwan's case as SMEs were dominant player in its post-war economic growth. Most of large firms' exports are promoted by its growing ODI in developing countries, particularly in China. While both countries have been relying on large firms' exports for its economic growth during the post-industrial development period, wage dispersion between large companies and SMEs with a bigger workforce has enlarged the income inequality. The government policy measures so far do not seem to reverse the gradually polarized economic structure.

Keywords Taiwan's small and medium enterprises • South Korea's small and medium enterprises • Asian financial crisis • Global financial crisis • Domestic employment

Taiwan's SMEs played an important role in its export-led economic development in the 1970s and 1980s. During this period, large companies focused on the production of intermediate goods for SME manufacturing destined for export (Lee and Hsiao 2014; Yu 2002). Hence, while SMEs were a heavyweight in Taiwan's exports, large firms were more important for Taiwan's domestic production. By contrast, South Korean chaebols

M.-H. Chiang, *Post-Industrial Development in East Asia*,
https://doi.org/10.1007/978-981-13-0274-9_3

have dominated the country's exports since its post-war industrialization. The SMEs in South Korea specialized in making products mainly for domestic consumption and generally in product areas that did not compete with chaebols (Feenstra and Hamilton 2006). Although the importance of SMEs in both countries' exports was different, SMEs have all accounted for a large portion of domestic employment. In this regard, SMEs have been important in maintaining social stability and cohesion in both countries. With the rise of domestic labor cost and protectionist measures from Western countries, Taiwan's export-oriented SMEs encountered tremendous challenges since the 1980s. Meanwhile, South Korean SMEs also suffered from the wages hike and growing foreign competition after the gradual economic liberalization. China's economic opening up provided new opportunities for the SMEs from both countries. As mentioned in Chap. 2, SMEs were the pioneers in Taiwan's and South Korea's ODI in China. However, the strategy of relocating factories to China to maintain their products' competitiveness did not last long. With China's mounting production cost and industrial upgrading, SMEs in labor-intensive manufacturing production can no longer profit from investing in China anymore.

The purpose of this chapter is to investigate the development of Taiwanese and South Korean SMEs and their contributions to the economy in the last two decades. The analysis of SME development could also provide insight on the expansion of large firms in both countries at the same time. In general, SMEs are more vulnerable to global economic fluctuations vis-à-vis large companies. With less resources and capacity to innovate, SMEs have gradually lost their competitiveness in this increasingly globalized world. Given their importance in domestic employment, the governments in Taiwan and South Korea have been making effort to develop SMEs during the era of globalization. To assess the diverse development of SMEs and their importance in the economy in both countries, this chapter is organized as follows. The first section provides a general overview of both countries' SMEs, including the definition and importance in their respective economies. The second and the third sections expound on the importance of SMEs in both the manufacturing and services sectors. The fourth section assesses the future prospects for SMEs by comparing the main policy initiatives aimed at promoting SME development in both countries. Finally, the main findings and conclusion of future prospects for SMEs are presented.

SMEs in Taiwan's and South Korea's Economy: A Comparison

Definitions of SMEs

Taiwan SME definition has experienced several revisions over the last few decades. According to the most updated definition in 2009, SMEs in manufacturing, construction, mining, and quarrying sectors refer to companies which hire less than 200 people, with paid-up capital amounting to less than NT$80 million (about US$2.5 million). SMEs in agriculture, electricity and gas supply, and services refer to companies which hire less than 100 people and with sales revenue in the previous year of below NT$100 million (about US$3.2 million) (Table 3.1). South Korea's definition of an SME also varies by sector. Compared with Taiwan's definition, the classification for SMEs by sector in South Korea is more specific. The manufacturing sectors with less than 300 workers and annual sales less than US$8 million are categorized as SMEs. For mining, construction, and transportation, the criterion is sales of less than US$3 million. For the large retail stores, hotel, recreational condominium operations, and so on, the benchmark for sales revenue is greater, with US$30 million or less. The more detailed definition is given in Table 3.1.

Table 3.1 Comparison of SMEs' definitions in Taiwan and South Korea

	Taiwan		*South Korea*	
	No. of workers	*Paid-up capital or sales*	*No. of workers*	*Capital and sales*
Manufacturing, construction, mining and quarrying sectors	Less than 200	Paid-up capital worth NT$80 million or less	n/a	
Agriculture, electricity and gas supply, and services	Less than 100	Sales worth NT$100 million or less		

(*continued*)

Table 3.1 (continued)

	Taiwan		*South Korea*	
	No. of workers	*Paid-up capital or sales*	*No. of workers*	*Capital and sales*
Manufacturing	n/a		Less than 300	Capital worth US$8 million or less
Mining, construction, and transportation			Less than 300	Capital worth US$3 million or less
Large general retail stores, hotel, recreational condominium operation, communications, information processing and other computer-related industries, engineering service, hospital, and broadcasting			Less than 300	Sales worth US$30 million or less
Seed and seedling production, fishing, electrical, gas and waterworks, medical and orthopedic products, wholesales, fuel and related products wholesales, mail order sale, door-to-door sale, tour agency, warehouses and transportation related service, professional, science and technology service, business support service, movie, amusement and theme park operation			Less than 200	Sales worth US$20 million or less
Wholesale and product intermediation, machinery equipment rent for industrial use, R&D for natural science, public performance, news provision, botanical garden, zoo and natural parks, waste water treatment, waste disposal, and cleaning-related service			Less than 100	Sales worth US$10 million or less
Other sectors			Less than 50	Sales worth US$5 million or less

Source: Small and Medium Enterprise Administration (2013), OECD (2016)

There are several features of SMEs in Taiwan and South Korea. First, the density of SMEs in both countries is similar. According to the official statistics, Taiwan has nearly 1.4 million SMEs whereas South Korea has 3.5 million in 2014. Divided by the total population, there are 6.1 SMEs per 100 people in Taiwan while in South Korea, the ratio is 6.9. Second, the SMEs in both countries are overwhelmingly dominated by their services sectors. Among the 1.4 million SMEs in Taiwan, 88 percent are in services, 10.6 percent in manufacturing sectors, and less than 1 percent in the agricultural and mineral sectors. Similarly in South Korea, 89.3 percent of SMEs are in services and 10.7 percent in manufacturing sectors in 2012 (Suh 2014). Another striking feature is that the majority of SMEs in both countries are very small in terms of the number of employees. According to OECD, 93.2 percent of South Korean SMEs are micro enterprises which employ up to nine employees (OECD 2016). The figure for Taiwan's micro enterprise with fewer than five employees in 2011 is 79 percent of the total number of SMEs (SMEA 2015).

Changing Importance of SMEs in Taiwan's and South Korea's Economies

SMEs have consistently accounted for a dominant share in Taiwan and South Korea's total number of companies. In 1995, 98 percent of companies in Taiwan were SMEs. In 2015, the ratio changed only slightly to 97.7 percent. In South Korea, the ratio also changed slightly from 99.1 percent to 99.9 percent during the same period (Table 3.2). With the growing number of firms, the insignificant change in percentages shows the number of both SMEs and large firms could have increased at the same time. As such, it indicates that there could be an increasing competition between SMEs as well as between SMEs and large companies. Nonetheless, the growing number of SMEs in Taiwan and South Korea did not make them more important in the economy. Instead, SME contribution to both countries' exports has gradually declined over the last two decades.

As shown in Table 3.2, SMEs once contributed to 50.7 percent of Taiwan's exports in 1995 but this declined to only 15.2 percent in 2015. The turning point was the AFC during 1997 and 1998. In 1997, the shares of SMEs in Taiwan's total exports dropped sharply to 26.6 percent, from 49.8 percent in the previous year. According to the official survey, 86 percent of SMEs reported the decline in their business profit as being due

Table 3.2 Comparison of SMEs' shares in exports and employment in Taiwan and South Korea 1995–2015

	Taiwan			*South Korea*		
	Share in total no. of firms	*Share in exports*	*Share in employment*	*Share in total no. of firms*	*Share in exports*	*Share in employment*
1995	98.0	50.7	79.8	99.1	39.6	n/a
1996	98.0	49.8	78.6	99.1	41.8	n/a
1997	97.8	26.6	78.4	99.1	41.8	n/a
1998	97.8	23.8	78.2	99.2	42.6	75.3
1999	97.7	21.1	78.3	99.3	n/a	n/a
2000	98.1	20.0	78.1	99.2	37.0	80.6
2001	98.2	20.7	77.7	99.7	42.9	84.4
2002	97.8	19.3	77.9	99.8	42.0	86.5
2003	97.8	18.1	77.6	99.8	42.2	86.8
2004	97.7	17.1	77.2	99.8	35.6	86.4
2005	97.8	17.6	76.9	99.9	32.4	87.8
2006	97.8	17.9	76.7	99.9	32.0	87.3
2007	97.7	17.1	77.1	99.9	32.0	88.4
2008	97.7	17.4	76.6	99.9	21.1	87.7
2009	97.9	16.9	78.5	99.9	21.1	87.7
2010	97.7	16.2	78.1	99.9	21.1	86.8
2011	97.6	16.3	77.9	99.9	18.3	86.9
2012	97.8	17.7	78.1	99.9	18.8	87.7
2013	97.6	14.5	78.3	99.9	17.1	87.5
2014	97.6	14.6	78.3	99.9	18.0	87.9
2015	97.7	15.2	78.2	n/a	18.3	n/a

Source: Small and Medium Enterprise Administration, various years; KOSIS; Gregory et al. (2002)

to the AFC. Forty-five percent of SMEs reported the decrease of exports. The government responded with greater financial loans and human resource training for SMEs and encouraged SMEs to conduct R&D (Small and Medium Enterprise Administration 1999). The policy measures aimed at alleviating the impact from the AFC did not seem to enhance competitiveness of SMEs in exports. After the crisis, the share of SMEs in Taiwan's total exports continued to fall from 21.1 percent in 1999 to the lowest 14.5 percent in 2013. As a result, most of Taiwan's SMEs turned to rely on the domestic market as their main source of revenue. However, the sluggish domestic economy in recent years suggests that profits of SMEs could be limited. In contrast to their decreasing share in Taiwan's exports, the share of SMEs in Taiwan's employment has not changed much. About 77–79 percent of Taiwan's workers have been employed by SMEs in the last two decades. Although the SMEs play an important role in providing job opportunities domestically, the short life span (7–13 years) indicates the unstable nature of jobs offered. In other words, nearly 80 percent of workers in Taiwan employed by SMEs are under pressure of potential unemployment at any time.

South Korean SMEs were also severely impacted by the AFC. The number of SMEs that succumbed to bankruptcy rose from 11,600 in 1996 to 17,200 in 1997 and 22,800 in 1998 (Gregory et al. 2002). Some SMEs in manufacturing went bankrupt because the large companies they traded with became insolvent (Suh 2014). The post-crisis policy reform focusing on corporate and financial sector restructuring with further development of SMEs was initiated under Kim Dae-Jung's government. Despite the impact from the AFC, the share of South Korean SMEs in the country's total exports did not change a lot. The chaebols' deteriorating business after the crisis might have allowed importance of SMEs in exports to remain relatively unaffected. South Korean SMEs accounted for 41.8 percent of the country's exports in 1998 and this declined to 37 percent in 2000 and climbed to 42 percent in 2001. Nonetheless, their shares in the country's exports started to decline sharply after the GFC. As shown in Table 3.2, the exports made by South Korean SMEs shrunk from 32 percent in 2007 to 21.1 percent in 2008 and further declined to 18.3 percent in 2015. The quick fall of SMEs in South Korea's total export shares can be explained by the chaebols' growing export business after the GFC. Chaebols' increasing exports of intermediate goods were supported by their large ODI in developing countries for final product assembly. In 2010, exports by the 30 largest chaebols accounted for 84 percent of South Korea's overseas shipments (Bloomberg, 21 December 2012). In particular, the share of exports made by Samsung, the largest chaebol in the ICT industry, increased from 13 percent of South Korea's total exports in 1987 to 28 percent by 2012 (The Washington Post, 9 December 2012).

South Korean chaebols' growing exports made them even more important in South Korea's economy. Sales revenue generated by the top five chaebols in South Korea was equivalent to 58 percent of the country's GDP in 2015, increasing from 37 percent in 2008 and 45 percent in 2009. Foreign countries accounted for a large portion of the chaebols' sales revenue. According to a joint research, 86 percent of Samsung's sales were generated from its overseas markets and only 14 percent came from its domestic market in 2013. The overseas market also dominates in the cases of Hyundai Motor and LG (Graduate School of International Studies, Seoul National University; Columbia Centre on Sustainable Investment, Columbia University 2015).

Following the chaebols' business growth in overseas markets, foreign employees took important shares in some chaebols' employment profile. As such, the chaebols' contribution to domestic employment did not develop in tandem with their increasing business. This explains the increasing share of SMEs in domestic employment from 75.3 percent in 1998 to 87.9 percent in 2014 (Table 3.2). Despite their greater importance in offering jobs to domestic workers, the limited profit margin of SMEs constrains their financial resources to upgrade the industry and hire more qualified workers with better remuneration. Many young South Koreans today would rather stay unemployed than work at SMEs for inferior wages. That is one of the reasons for the higher unemployment rate for workers aged between 15 and 29 (9.5 percent in January 2016). Wage dispersion between large companies and SMEs with a bigger workforce has also enlarged the income inequality in the country. More discussion about the enlarging income inequality is discussed in Chap. 6.

Comparison of SMEs in Taiwan's and South Korea's Manufacturing Sectors

The shrinking importance of SMEs in Taiwan's economy is obvious in the manufacturing sectors. Here are some figures to illustrate. First, the number of SMEs in Taiwan's total number of manufacturing companies declined slightly from 97.8 percent in 1997 to 96.2 percent in 2015 (Table 3.3). However, in absolute numbers, Taiwan's SMEs in manufacturing sectors dwindled from its peak of 158,252 in 1997 to 142,686 in 1999. The number continued to decline to 132,354 in 2006 and recovered only slightly to 147,404 in 2014. Second, SMEs in manufacturing sectors contributed to 60 percent of Taiwan's export in 1990. The ratio declined sharply to 23.4 percent in 1997 and deteriorated further to 15.4 percent in 2015. On the other hand, the shares of SME domestic sales revenue increased clearly from 37.3 percent to 42.5 percent. Third, share of SMEs in Taiwan's total number of paid employees has decreased from 78.5 percent in 1997 to 70.2 percent in 2015. During the same period, their share in Taiwan's employment also dropped from 81.3 percent to

Table 3.3 Taiwan SME in manufacturing sectors 1997–2015

	No. of companies	*Exports*	*Domestic sales*	*Paid employees*	*Employment*
1997	97.8	23.4	37.3	78.5	81.3
1998	97.5	20.5	35.6	77.2	80.0
1999	97.3	17.4	34.7	77.6	80.4
2000	97.5	15.8	35.2	77.3	80.0
2001	97.4	16.6	35.2	77.3	79.9
2002	97.7	15.4	35.7	76.8	79.4
2003	97.0	19.8	46.1	76.6	79.2
2004	96.9	18.9	44.0	75.8	78.4
2005	96.9	20.4	43.3	74.4	77.0
2006	96.7	19.3	42.2	73.3	75.9
2007	96.6	18.4	40.6	74.1	76.7
2008	96.5	18.7	40.3	73.3	75.9
2009	96.4	17.7	40.1	73.1	75.7
2010	96.3	18.2	40.8	71.8	74.3
2011	96.2	18.7	40.5	70.6	73.2
2012	96.2	20.2	40.8	70.5	73.0
2013	96.1	14.7	40.1	71.0	73.5
2014	96.2	14.8	40.8	70.7	73.0
2015	96.2	15.4	42.5	70.2	72.5

Source: Small and Medium Enterprise Administration, various issues
Unit: As % of total in manufacturing sectors

72.5 percent. Overall, Taiwanese SMEs in manufacturing sectors have contributed less and less in both total employment and exports. However, they have taken greater shares in domestic sales.

The greater cooperative network between SMEs and large companies explains the former's decreasing export values. Since 1984, the Taiwanese government has started promoting the production network between SMEs and large companies. Large companies became the center of production for exports while SMEs were the suppliers of components and intermediate goods to large firms. As SMEs lacked capacity in R&D and marketing capabilities, the integration with large firms allowed the SMEs to concentrate only on manufacturing. At the same time, large firms could focus on R&D and high-value-added production. However, there is no exact figure about how much of output from SMEs is destined for large companies' exports. According to Taiwan's Corporate Synergy Development Center, about 20 percent of total SMEs in manufacturing sectors, ranging from vehicles, aerospace, machinery, electronic products, and consumer goods act as satellite factories to large firms (CSD Review 2014). Indeed, despite the declining shares in Taiwan's exports, overall SME sales revenues in absolute terms, including export revenue and domestic sales revenue, have increased. Shares of SMEs in total companies' sales revenue (including large firms and SMEs) have remained relatively unchanged over the last two decades. The large companies' export expansion might have made SMEs less important in Taiwan's exports. On the other hand, the integration with large firms has allowed SMEs to achieve greater domestic market sales. Other factors such as Taiwan's limited FTA network and the growing local procurement of Taiwanese companies in China also explain the declining importance of SMEs in Taiwan's total exports.

The importance of the SMEs in South Korea's manufacturing sectors is shown in Table 3.4. In 1999, SMEs with fewer than 299 employees (including SMEs with 10–99 and 100–299 employees) comprised 45 percent of value of shipment and this percentage increased slightly to 46 percent in 2014. However, the value-added production has clearly declined from 46 percent to 40.5 percent during the same period. On the other hand, large companies with more than 300 employees took greater share in value-added production in 2014 (59.4 percent) than in 1999 (54 percent). The SMEs in manufacturing sectors with 10–99 employees have contributed the most to domestic employment. Their shares in total number of workers have increased from 51.4 percent in 1999 to 55.7 percent in 2014. During the same period, the number of workers hired by SMEs with 100–299 employees remained unchanged (from 18.4 percent to 18.8 percent). The large companies with more than 300 employees have contributed the least to the domestic employment. The shares of total number of workers hired by large companies declined clearly from 30.2 percent in 1999 to 25.5 percent in 2014.

The weak Japanese yen and soft external demand have badly hurt the SMEs in manufacturing sectors in recent years. Exports by SMEs fell 3.9 percent between 2009 and 2013 according to a report by the Korea Small Business Institute. The Korea International Trade Association's survey in 2014 showed that 95 percent of SME business was negatively impacted by the weak yen (Kang 2014). The business disintegration between South Korean SMEs and chaebols in manufacturing production might explain why the SMEs did not benefit from chaebols' business expansion. South Korean chaebols bought most of the industrial inputs from their own subsidiaries, instead of from other SMEs. For example,

Table 3.4 South Korean SME and large companies in manufacturing sectors in 1999, 2003, 2009 and 2014

	Number of establishment	*Value of shipments*	*Value-added*	*Number of workers*
		1999		
10–99	93.2	27.2	27.6	51.4
100–299	5.3	17.8	18.4	18.4
300 and more	1.4	54.9	54.0	30.2
		2003		
10–99	93.9	30.4	31.6	55.2
100–299	4.9	17.7	18.4	18.5
300 and more	1.2	51.9	50.0	26.3
		2009		
10–99	93.8	28.9	26.5	54.3
100–299	5.2	16.3	14.5	19.2
300 and more	1.0	54.7	58.9	26.5
		2014		
10–99	93.9	29.3	27.0	55.7
100–299	5.1	16.7	13.5	18.8
300 and more	1.0	53.9	59.4	25.5

Source: KOSIS
Unit: As % of total in manufacturing sectors

Samsung Electronics made 80 percent of its 69 trillion won (US$68.19 billion) in purchases in 2011 from its subsidiaries. A total of 55 percent of purchases were from overseas subsidiaries and 45 percent was from their domestic ones. In fact, South Korea also tried to strengthen the competitiveness of SMEs through promoting cooperation between large firms and SMEs since the 1990s (Suh 2014). The continuous disintegration between chaebols and SMEs showed the ineffectiveness of the policy. In addition, a considerable number of large companies in the area of manufacturing invested more money in foreign subsidiaries than domestic subsidiaries (Kwak 2014). Although South Korea has a more extensive FTA network, many Korean SMEs did not utilize the FTAs to expand their exports. Most of them do not have enough staff to deal with FTA businesses and lack the professional expertise in trade practice and business activities (Cheong 2014).

Comparison of SMEs in Taiwan's and South Korea's Services

Table 3.5 shows the breakdown information of Taiwan SMEs in services. In each services sector, the share of SMEs in terms of number of companies, employment, domestic sales, and exports are displayed. The main findings from the table are as follows. First, like in the manufacturing sectors, most of the companies in services are SMEs. At least 96 percent of service firms in Taiwan are SMEs except for financial services. Second, the employment shares of SMEs in most of the services are higher than their employment shares in manufacturing sectors. Over 90 percent of employment in construction, wholesale and retail trade, accommodation and restaurants, real estate, support services, and other services are provided by SMEs. In comparison, SMEs hired the fewest number of local workers in education services (36.7 percent). This can be reasoned by the fact that most of the teachers and administration staff are working with large schools and universities. Similarly, SMEs accounted for relatively less employment in healthcare and social services (50.1 percent). This is

Table 3.5 Taiwan SMEs in service sectors in 2015

	No. of companies	*Employment*	*Domestic sales*	*Exports*
Construction services	99.0	98.1	66.2	26.7
Wholesale and retail trade	97.5	96.1	34.6	17.3
Transportation and storage	96.4	73.9	32.8	2.5
Accommodation and restaurants	99.6	97.2	70.0	10.9
Information and telecommunication services	96.2	69.5	11.4	6.9
Financial services	86.4	77.0	8.5	8.4
Real estate	95.9	96.1	21.3	27.4
Professional, scientific, and technology services	98.4	80.7	37.5	5.4
Supporting services	98.3	90.9	28.1	16.8
Education services	99.3	36.7	70.6	37.3
Healthcare and social services	98.1	50.1	25.3	4.2
Art, entertainment, and leisure services	99.5	80.8	59.0	98.4
Other services	99.8	98.5	54.0	3.7

Source: White Paper on Small and Medium Enterprises in Taiwan, various issues
Unit: As % of total in each sector

because the healthcare and social services are usually operated either by government or by large conglomerates. SMEs in higher value-added services such as professional, scientific and technology services (80.7 percent) and financial services (77 percent) accounted for relatively lower percentages of domestic employment compared to other sectors. Third, the SMEs have generated 70.6 percent of domestic sales in education services despite their lower percentage in employment. Unlike the public schools and universities, SMEs in education services like cram schools are profit-oriented. SMEs in accommodation and restaurants (70 percent), construction services (66.2 percent), and arts, entertainment, and leisure services (59 percent) also accounted for a large share of total domestic sales. The relatively higher shares in domestic sales indicated heavy reliance on the domestic market. Finally, like in the manufacturing sectors, SMEs in services accounted for a smaller share in Taiwan's total export values. The exception is SMEs in arts, entertainment, and leisure services which accounted for 98.4 percent of the total exports. Overall, SMEs in services take a dominant share in domestic employment. However, their share in domestic sales is relatively smaller and the weight in exports can be said to be insignificant.

Due to the limited profits for SMEs in both domestic and international markets, many people in Taiwan doubted the benefits that SMEs would gain from the service trade deal signed with China in 2013. As mentioned in Chap. 2, the CSSTA would open up 64 industries within the services sector in Taiwan to China and 80 industries in China to Taiwan. The opening up of China's service sectors to Taiwan's investment is expected to diversify Taiwan service firms from the small domestic market to China's giant market. Nonetheless, as sectors that China fully opens up to Taiwan's investment (sectors in Taiwan which remain closed to the Chinese) are mostly the high-value-added sectors (such as auditing and accounting, real estate services, construction services, and hospitals), the concern is the potential brain drain in these sectors to China. On the contrary, Taiwan has to open its low-value-added sectors such as hair and cosmetics to China (sectors in China which remain closed to the Taiwan firms), giving SMEs in the low-value-added sectors not only no opportunity to take advantage of China's booming market but also potential competition from China.

Like in Taiwan, South Korean SMEs also make the most important contribution to employment in domestic services sector. In particular, 95.3 percent of employment in hotels and restaurants are hired by SMEs with 1–49 workers (Table 3.6). SMEs with fewer than 49 workers in education (91.2 percent), membership organizations, repairing and other personal services activities (91 percent), wholesale and retail (89 percent), and real estate (87.7 percent) also accounted for relatively higher

Table 3.6 South Korean SMEs and large companies in service sectors in 2014

	Number of establishment	*Number of workers*	*Annual sales*
Wholesale and retail			
1–49 workers	99.7	89.0	76.1
50 and over	0.3	11.0	23.9
Hotels and restaurants			
1–49 workers	99.9	95.3	89.3
50 and over	0.1	4.7	10.7
Sewage, wastewater treatment, recycling, and restoration activities of environment			
1–49 workers	97.0	76.7	79.1
50 and over	3.0	23.3	20.9
Publishing, motion picture, broadcasting telecommunication, and information service activities			
1–49 workers	95.7	49.0	34.2
50 and over	4.3	51.0	65.8
Real estate activities			
1–49 workers	99.7	87.7	67.9
50 and over	0.3	12.3	32.1
Business facilities management and business support services			
1–49 workers	92.9	29.6	45.7
50 and over	7.1	70.4	54.3
Education			
1–49 workers	99.7	91.0	81.6
50 and over	0.3	9.0	18.4
Human health and social work activities			
1–49 workers	97.2	60.9	48.7
50 and over	2.8	39.1	51.3
Arts, sports, and recreation related services			
1–49 workers	99.3	73.3	51.0
50 and over	0.7	26.7	49.0
Membership organizations, repairing, and other personal services activities			
1–49 workers	99.8	91.2	86.6
50 and over	0.2	8.8	13.4

Source: KOSIS
Unit: As % of total in each sector

percentages of employment vis-à-vis companies with more than 50 workers. In contrast, SMEs in business facilities management and business support services hired 29.6 percent as compared to large companies with more than 50 workers, which hired 70 percent of total workers. In terms of annual sales, SMEs in most of the services sector industries accounted for more than half of total sales except publishing, motion picture, broadcasting telecommunication and information service activities, business facilities management and business support services, and human health and social work activities.

Due to the high concentration of SMEs in wholesale and retail, accommodation and restaurant, the trend of second- and third-generation chaebol families opening bakeries and other small food outlets in recent years raised concerns about a threat to the livelihoods of small store owners. With the support of their parents' business empires, these chaebol-linked shops were set up in hotels, department stores, and other large buildings with good locations and sales. While the retail business run by chaebols heirs and offspring flourished, the number of bakeries run by self-employed individuals plunged significantly from about 18,000 in 2003 to around 4000 in 2011 according to the Korea Federation of Small and Medium Business (Kim 2012).

Comparing the Main SME Policies of Both Governments

As early as in 1966, a working group was established under Taiwan's Executive Yuan to support the development of SMEs. After several re-organizations, the Small and Medium Enterprises Administration (SMEA) under the Ministry of Economic Affairs was set up in 1981 to assist in SME development. The policy measures implemented by SMEA to facilitate SME's development have evolved over time. "The Rule for Promotion of Small and Medium Enterprises" was promulgated in 1967. In 1991, the Rule was turned into law with an aim to provide a wider range of assistance to SMEs, such as provision of loans, market promotion, labor training, upgrading technology, forming strategic alliance, and so on (Hu and Schive 1998).

At present, Taiwan's SMEs policy aims to construct a business-friendly environment, facilitate the use of high technology in business operations, enhance business management, integrate the financial mechanism of SMEs, and build a platform for enterprise start-up and incubation. The government's financial support for SME development has mainly been via financial loans from banks. In 2015, 68 percent of SMEs acquired financial funding through the banking loans, followed by nearly 20 percent of equities and 12 percent of domestic corporate bonds, short-term bills, and asset-backed securities (SMEA 2015). Another important policy is to encourage SME innovation and help them adapt to globalization. In view of insufficient financial resources, the Taiwanese government has established several non-profit R&D institutes to facilitate technology transfer to SMEs. The most noticeable ones are the Industrial Technology & Research Institute (ITRI) and Hsinchu Science-based Industrial Park (HSIP). Starting from 1996, ITRI has provided joint research and start-up enterprise incubator services. HSIP provides physical infrastructure that allows firms to be located in the same vicinity, thus facilitating integration of industry and creating competitive advantages for individual firms (Chen et al. 2013). In order to assist SMEs to innovate and start their business, the Taiwanese government also set up incubation centers, providing incubation services ranging from creativity and innovation to starting enterprises, establishing a comprehensive incubation system for individuals intending to start their own enterprises. Since 1997, 130 incubation centers have been set up in several universities in Taiwan. A total of 11,213 SMEs were developed through aid from the incubation centers. Eighty-seven SMEs were listed on the stock market (SMEA 2016). Other policy initiatives such as the provision of financial loans for new start-ups, assistance in marketing and commercializing the products, and aid to adapt to the uses of information technology have been implemented. Nonetheless, the assistance offered by the government to strengthen SME competitiveness was not always considered useful (Chen and Parker 2007). The diverse difficulties among SMEs could have made it very difficult for the policies to adequately address each company's demand.

The South Korean government's financial support to SME development started as early as in 1979. However, due to the limited flow of information, very few SMEs benefited from the official promotional program in the beginning. In the 1990s, many protection-oriented measures were replaced by competition-based measures, following market liberalization. South Korea's SME policy turned to focus on fostering innovative SMEs (Suh 2014). In 1995, the Small and Medium Business Administration (SMBA) was inaugurated to assist SME development in South Korea (Gregory et al. 2002). Nowadays, the objectives of South Korean SME policy are to boost start-up firms, improve competitiveness, facilitate business transformation, and promote fair competition. The specific measures to assist SMEs include financial support, tax reduction, government funds, and grants (Suh 2014).

With continuous financial support from government, loans by commercial banks to SMEs increased from 13 percent of GDP in 1997 to 42 percent in 2009, but declined to 36 percent in 2012. However, the government's financial guarantees to financial institutions that loaned to SMEs have produced some side effects. On the one hand, they reduce incentives for financial institutions to improve their capacity for credit evaluation of SMEs. On the other hand, it allows weak companies to survive. Some SMEs may choose to remain small so as to stay eligible for public support (Jones and Kim 2014). Unlike Taiwan SMEs which relied on government-backed research institutions for new technology, most of the South Korean firms were independent, not relying upon transfer from the incumbent firms but rather hiring local engineers and building their own capabilities. In addition, they are not integrated with the supply chain network of foreign MNCs (Lee and Mathews 2012) unlike many Taiwanese SMEs. This might have constrained their capacity to upgrade their industries.

To resolve the enlarging gap between SMEs and chaebols in terms of productivity, the South Korean government shifted the SME policy direction from "protection and assistance" to building a stepping stone for "autonomy and competition" in the late 1990s. The South Korean government began to place the emphasis on business start-up with intensive knowledge and technology. For instance, in 1997, the government launched the SME Technology Innovation Development Programme to induce R&D activities of SMEs by subsidizing a proportion of the expenditure for new product development. In 1998, South Korea's SMBA introduced the Triangle of Technology Assistance for SMEs, which was designed to support the link between universities and SMEs. The industry-academy-research institute joint R&D was initiated to help SMEs to commercialize their innovative products. Since 2005, the technology R&D centers by industry-academia partnership have helped SMEs to utilize the facilities and human resources at universities. The government budgets for SME technology development also improved from 1618.9 billion won in 2011 to 1725.5 billion won in 2013 (Suh 2014). The assistance to SMEs did not come at the expense of large companies. Although the government's financial subsidies to SMEs increased 3.4 times in the 2002–2012 period, its financial support to large firms had a tenfold increase. In 2002, SMEs took up 81 percent of the government budget for promoting R&D

while large firms only 19 percent. In 2012 however, the SME share declined to 60 percent and that of large firms increased to 40 percent (Kang and Mah 2015).

In 2013, President Park announced plans to build a "Creative Economy" which aimed to promote a new growth model based on innovation and entrepreneurship. Nonetheless, such an "innovation-driven" economic growth only enhanced the country's reliance on chaebols which accounted for most of private R&D investments. Over the past few years, to become a new pioneer in biopharmaceutical manufacturing in the world, Samsung has made huge investment (US$2.74 billion) in production plants and research laboratories in biotechnology sectors in South Korea (Cheng and Lee *The Wall Street Journal*, 17 December 2015). Hyundai Motor Group has also announced in 2015 that it would spend US$73 billion over four years on expanding capacity, building new headquarters and developing new vehicles. About three quarters of the investment would be made within South Korea (*Reuters*, 6 January 2015a). LG also planned to invest more than 10 trillion won (US$8.71 billion) to build a large plant to produce panels using organic light-emitting diode (OLED) panels. The initial 1.84 trillion won will be used to build the plant in Paju, South Korea (*Reuters*, 26 November 2015b). Heavy investment in R&D is supposed to benefit South Korea's industrial upgrading and maintain its technology superiority ahead of its peers. Given the rich financial resources of chaebols, they are more capable of playing an important role in promoting South Korea's transformation into a more innovation- and high technology-driven economy in the long run.

In the face of economic slowdown in recent years, the South Korean government could not afford to abandon economic policies that are short-term and chaebol-oriented. In 2013, the Park administration announced reduction of tax audits on large corporations. Tax reduction was also offered for the chaebol practice of funneling work to affiliates as large companies often argued that strict regulations on funneling have sapped corporations' desire to invest (The Hankyoreh 2013). Like her predecessor, President Park also pardoned several tycoons' corruption charges, including SK and Samsung's chairmen, contradicting what she had promised during her election campaign. Although supporting measures for SMEs continued to remain in place, for the sake of South Korean economic growth, the government did not withdraw its pro-chaebol policies. Hence, SMEs continue to struggle when expanding their business in an economy largely dominated by chaebols.

Conclusion

The development of SMEs in Taiwan and South Korea over the last two decades can be summarized as follows. First, Taiwan's SMEs sectors have become more dependent on the domestic market than on exports. Unlike a few decades ago, large companies now play a more significant role in Taiwan's exports. This switchover between Taiwan's exports and domestic sales is particularly obvious in the manufacturing sectors. The global economic slowdown, growing foreign competition, Taiwan's minimum involvement in both bilateral and multilateral FTAs and the Taiwanese government's promotion of industrial integration between SMEs and large companies are reasons behind the declining importance of SMEs in Taiwan's exports. In particular, the government's effort to integrate SMEs and large companies in industrial production could have made SMEs turn to focus on the domestic market in support of large companies' production for exports. Unlike Taiwan, South Korea's exports have been dominated by the large companies from the start. Contribution by South Korean SMEs to exports did not have significant changes after the AFC as chaebols also suffered severely from the crisis. After the GFC, however, the importance of South Korean SMEs in exports clearly declined. Beyond the macroeconomic factors, the disintegration between large firms and SMEs in manufacturing production explained the sluggish SME exports whereas the large companies profited from their business expansion in overseas markets.

Second, despite the insignificant share in exports, SMEs made most of the contribution to domestic employment in both countries. Especially after the relocation of manufacturing sectors to other developing countries, many workers shifted to SMEs in services. Due to the importance of SMEs in providing jobs for local workers, Taiwan's service trade deal with China became controversial. The political implications notwithstanding, Taiwan does need foreign competition to improve its services sector's competitiveness. SMEs are often blamed for their short-sightedness and unwillingness/inability to take a long-term approach. The competition in the domestic market often led to cutthroat price competition. As such, SMEs can benefit from FDI to improve their service quality, management skills, and other business areas. In comparison, South Korean SMEs in services suffered not only from the foreign competition but also from chaebols' business extension to other industries within the services sector in recent years. In the face of the more globalized world, the governments in Taiwan and South Korea will have to construct a business-friendly environment for firms to compete.

Third, by comparing SME development in both Taiwan and South Korea, this chapter shows the imbalanced economic structures in both countries. After the AFC, both the Taiwanese and South Korean economies have undergone a structural change that resulted in greater polarization between large global market-oriented exporting firms and domestic market-oriented SMEs. In the process of recovery from the GFC, the large companies have been able to bounce back relatively quickly, unlike SMEs which appear to have been severely weakened by its effects. In South Korea, some of the policy measures intended to nurture SME development did not change the economic structure to be less chaebol-dominated. Instead, chaebols have grown much stronger than ever. The gap between chaebols and SMEs in terms of productivity, profitability, and competitiveness has increased as a result.

Finally, the presence of stronger large firms does not necessary mean the SMEs will not be able to survive. With large firms focusing more on international markets, economies of scale and capital-intensive production, SMEs could find their niche in the specialized, client-oriented and relatively labor-intensive fabrication. The governments' consistent efforts for revitalizing SMEs are important given their importance for domestic employment, economic diversification, and source of income for the vast majority of the two populations. With the changing international and domestic environment, the policy of both governments will have to evolve over time.

References

Bloomberg. (2012, December 21). Park presidency gives fighting chance to Korea's chaebols. Retrieved April 18, 2013, from http://www.bloomberg.com/news/2012-12-20/park-presidency-gives-fighting-chance-to-south-korea-s-chaebols.html

Chen, J., & Parker, D. (2007). Taiwan's textile and clothing SME response to globalization. *Journal of Asia-Pacific Business, 8*(2), 89–111.

Chen, C.-Y., Lin, Y.-L., & Chu, P.-Y. (2013). Facilitators of national innovation policy in a SME-dominated country: A case study of Taiwan. *Innovation: Management, Policy and Practice, 15*(4), 405–415.

Cheong, I. (2014). Korea's policy package for enhancing its FTA utilization and implications for Korea's policy. ERIA Discussion Paper Series. Retrieved July 10, 2017, from http://www.eria.org/ERIA-DP-2014-11.pdf

CSD Review. (2014). The corporate synergy development in Taiwan (zhong wei ti xi zai tai wan). No. 29, July 15. Retrieved February 28, 2018, from http://www.csd.org.tw/report/preview/84.html

Feenstra, R. C., & Hamilton, G. G. (2006). *Emergent economies, divergent paths: Economic organization and International Trade in South Korea and Taiwan.* New York: Cambridge University Press.

Graduate School of International Studies at Seoul National University and the Columbia Centre on Sustainable Investment at the Columbia University. (2015). The top 20 Korean multinationals: Changes and continued growth of foreign investment. Retrieved March 7, 2016, from http://ccsi.columbia.edu/files/2015/04/EMGP-Korea-Report-2015-report-on-2013-FINAL.pdf

Gregory, G., Harvie, C., & Lee, H.-H. (2002). Korean SMEs in the 21th century: Strategies, constraints and performance in a global economy. *Economic Papers, 21*(3), 64–79.

Hu, M.-H., & Schive, C. (1998). The changing competitiveness of Taiwan's manufacturing SMEs. *Small Business Economics, 11*(4), 315–326.

Jones, R. S., & Kim, M. (2014). Promoting the financial of SMEs and start-ups in Korea. *OECD Economics Department Working Paper.* No. 1162, 1–37.

Kang, T.-J. (2014). South Korea's SMEs struggle to compete. *Financial Times*, 25 November. Accessed 24 February 2016, from http://blogs.ft.com/beyond-brics/2014/11/25/south-koreas-smes-struggle-to-compete

Kang, H., & Mah, J. S. (2015). R&D policy for small and medium-sized enterprises in Korea. *Science, Technology & Society, 20*(1), 1–20.

Kim, S.-H. (2012). Korea's chaebol scion slammed for running coffee shops, Import Business. *The Korea Herald*, January 28. Retrieved February 23, 2016, from http://news.asiaone.com/News/AsiaOne%2BNews/Asia/Story/A1Story20120128-324406.html

Korean Statistical Information Service (KOSIS). Statistics Korea. Retrieved March 2, 2018., from http://kosis.kr/eng/

Kwak, J.-S. (2014). Chaebol getting more power as they contribute less to the economy. *The Hankyoreh*, July 9. Retrieved February 29, 2016, from http://english.hani.co.kr/arti/english_edition/e_business/646183.html

Lee, K., & Mathews, J. A. (2012). South Korea and Taiwan. In E. Amann & J. Cantwell (Eds.), *Innovative firms in emerging market countries.* Oxford: Oxford University Press.

Lee, Z.-r., & Hsiao, H.-H. M. (2014). Taiwan: SME-oriented capitalism in transition. In M. Witt & G. Redding (Eds.), *The Oxford handbook of Asian business system.* Oxford: Oxford University Press.

OECD. (2016). Korea. *Financing SMEs and Entrepreneurs 2016: An OECD Scoreboard.* Paris: OECD Publishing.

Reuters (2015a, January 6). Hyundai Motor Group says to invest $73 billion by 2018. Retrieved February 26, 2016, from http://www.reuters.com/article/us-hyundai-motor-investment-idUSKBN0KF0AS20150106

Reuters. (2015b, November 26). South Korea's LG display to invest $8.7 in new OLED plant. Retrieved November 26, 2015, from http://www.reuters.com/article/us-lg-display-investment-idUSKBN0TF2JY20151127

Small and Medium Enterprise Administration (Taiwan). (1999). *White Paper on small and medium enterprises (zhong xiao qi ye bai pi shu)*. Taipei: Ministry of Economic Affairs (Taiwan).

Small and Medium Enterprise Administration (Taiwan). (2013). *White Paper on small and medium enterprises (zhong xiao qi ye bai pi shu)*. Taipei: Ministry of Economic Affairs (Taiwan).

Small and Medium Enterprise Administration (Taiwan). (2015). *White Paper on small and medium enterprises (zhong xiao qi ye bai pi shu)*. Taipei: Ministry of Economic Affairs (Taiwan).

Small and Medium Enterprise Administration (Taiwan). (2016). Start-up and incubation (zhong xiao qi ye chuang xin yu cheng zhong xin). 29 April. Retrieved April 24, 2017, from http://www.moeasmea.gov.tw/ct.asp?xItem=625&ctNode=613&mp=1

Suh, J. (2014). *Korean Small Business: Development, current situation and priority for the future*. Seoul: Korea University Press.

The Hankyoreh (2013, August 4). Park administration bowing to chaebol pressure on reform measures. Retrieved February 22, 2016, from http://english.hani.co.kr/arti/english_edition/e_business/598200.html

The Wall Street Journal. (2015, December 17). Samsung's bet on biotechnology is test for heir apparent. Retrieved February 26, 2016, from http://www.wsj.com/articles/samsungs-bet-on-biotechnology-is-test-for-heir-apparent-1450386875

The Washington Post. (2012, December 9). In South Korea, the Republic of Samsung. Retrieved April 18, 2013, from http://www.wpost.com/world/in-s-korea-the-republic-of-samsung/2012/12/09/71215420-3de1-11e2-bca3-aadc9b7e29c5_story_2.html

Yu, T.-s. (2002). In J. S. Lee & C. Schieve (Eds.), *Taiwan's economic development and the role of SMEs*. Taipei: The Chung-Hua Institute for Economic Research.

CHAPTER 4

Comparing Governments' Policies in Promoting Economic Growth (I): Industrial Upgrading Policies

Abstract Both Taiwan and South Korean governments have tried to maintain high economic growth rates through industrial upgrading at home. Over the past two decades, their exports have been shifting from manufactured goods to commodities with higher technology and capital intensity. However, the greater exports of high-technology products do not necessarily mean a success in industrial upgrading. Both countries have continued to rely on importing foreign technology, particularly from the US and Japan. At the same time, both are facing growing competition from their Chinese counterparts. Taiwan and South Korea's economic growth prospect could become feeble if they are not able to maintain technology superiority vis-à-vis China.

Keywords Industrial upgrading policies • Information and communication technology (ICT) sector • Services sector • High-value-added products • R&D expenditure

Industrial upgrading, an essential contributor to economic development, refers to the shift of industrial structure to higher value-added production. To maintain economic growth, the Taiwanese and South Korean governments have been promoting industrial upgrading since several decades ago. In Taiwan, "Status for Industry's Upgrading" legislation was enacted as early as in 1979. The ICT sectors were the main

M.-H. Chiang, *Post-Industrial Development in East Asia*,
https://doi.org/10.1007/978-981-13-0274-9_4

target for upgrading. The Taiwanese government has encouraged the development of ICT industry since the 1970s with measures including the acquisition of foreign technology for introduction to local companies, establishment of science parks as well as promotion and expansion of ICT-related education. In addition to the government's effort, FDI and associated technology transfer particularly from the US MNCs have facilitated the entry of Taiwanese firms into different ICT subsectors over time, from electronic assembly to manufacturing computer-related products, integrated circuit (IC), and liquid crystal devices (LCD). As for South Korea, its Science & Technology (S&T) policy initiated since the 1960s was the foundation of its industrial development. With the establishment of government-funded research institutes and some preferential measures for R&D development, a system that allowed Korea to absorb and adapt foreign technology in support of its industrialization was formulated (OECD 2009). The private sectors also began to muster their own applied research capacity (Campbell 2012). The high level of R&D spending by large companies has been another essential factor in the development of South Korea's high-technology sectors. In sum, the industrialization of Taiwan and Korea in the early phase was a process of learning how to absorb and improve on imported foreign technologies.

This chapter investigates the industrial upgrading in Taiwan and South Korea in the past two recent decades. After post-war industrialization, how have Taiwan and South Korea continued to develop their economies through industrial upgrading? To address the question, the following section first introduces the economic structural changes in Taiwan and South Korea. The large presence of services in both countries is not the strengthening of the services sector. It is a result of the relatively weak manufacturing production in the economy. Second, despite its small share in the economy, the manufacturing sector remains the key driver for economic growth. To maintain the competitiveness of manufacturing exports, both governments have been actively promoting industrial upgrading. The third and the fourth sections examine the main industrial development policies in Taiwan and South Korea. The assessment of Taiwan and Korea's technical capacity after the industrial upgrading initiatives is presented in the fifth section. The conclusion will sum up the main finding and arguments raised in this chapter.

Manufacturing-Driven Economic Growth Despite Large Presence of Services in the Economy

Taiwan's and South Korea's economic structures have changed dramatically compared to the post-war industrialization period. As shown in Table 4.1, in 1986, the manufacturing sector accounted for 39.4 percent of Taiwan's GDP. The ratio declined to only 25.5 percent in 1996 and gradually grew to 30.2 percent in 2016. Accompanying the declining share of the manufacturing sector is the growing importance of services. In 1986, services accounted for 55.1 percent of Taiwan's GDP and this increased to nearly 68 percent in 2016. In South Korea, the importance of the manufacturing sector in GDP has remained relatively unchanged, about 24–28 percent from 1986 to 2016 according to the official statistics. The increasing share of services is mainly because of the shrinkage of agricultural sectors. The share of agricultural and mining sectors in South Korea's GDP declined from 12.8 percent in 1986 to 2.4 percent in 2016. During the same period, the weight of services increased from 59.4 percent to 71.6 percent.

Nevertheless, the growing importance of services in Taiwan and South Korea does not mean the strengthening of the services sector. In Taiwan's case, it is due to the weakening manufacturing sector that allowed for services to expand their share in the economy. This is evidenced by the slowing down of economic growth in recent years despite the greater share of services in GDP. When Taiwan experienced high economic growth during the post-war industrialization period, the manufacturing sector accounted for the largest share in GDP. It was the exports of manufacturing goods that contributed to the high economic growth. The booming manufacturing

Table 4.1 Comparison of Taiwan and South Korea's GDP by sector

	Taiwan			*South Korea*		
	Agriculture	*Manufacturing*	*Services*	*Agriculture*	*Manufacturing*	*Services*
1986	5.5	39.4	55.1	12.8	27.8	59.4
1996	3.0	25.5	71.5	4.4	22.2	73.5
2006	1.6	27.7	70.7	2.9	28.3	68.7
2016	1.8	30.2	68.0	2.4	26.6	71.6

Source: National Statistics (2017), National Development Council (Taiwan) (2002, 2016), KOSIS

sector also supported the development of services at home. However, when the manufacturing sector began gradually hollowing out after the relocation of factories abroad, the economy lost its engine for growth from the manufacturing sector. Meanwhile, the services sector is not able to replace manufacturing as the new engine for economic growth. Despite the declining share of the manufacturing sector in GDP, Taiwan still depends on manufacturing products as the main source of economic growth. This can be seen from Taiwan's net exports, an essential component of economic growth. Taiwan's net exports in manufacturing goods have been in surplus whereas its net exports in services have been in deficit. Similarly, although services accounted for a large share in Korea's GDP, it is the net exports in goods rather than services that contributed to the economic growth.

One important reason for weak services in supporting Taiwan's and South Korea's economies is that the services sectors in these two countries have been relatively small scale and domestically oriented. This is very different from Hong Kong and Singapore, where their internationally competitive services sectors contribute significantly to their economic development. In contrast, Taiwan's and Korea's services have been mainly for domestic consumption, low in terms of value-added and non-tradable. The roles of Hong Kong and Singapore as important transit ports for the grand markets of China and Southeast Asia, respectively, are also essential reasons for their more significant development of trade in services.

The need for industrial upgrading

Since services are too weak to stimulate economic growth, the manufacturing sector has remained important in developing the economy. However, Taiwan's and South Korea's exports of manufacturing goods have encountered tremendous difficulties in recent years. Insufficient industrial upgrading has been considered to be an important reason for the declining exports. As shown in Fig. 4.1, the annual export growth rates in Taiwan and South Korea have been developing quite similarly over the last two decades. The two countries' exports declined sharply due to the AFC in 1998, the technology bubble burst in 2001, and GFC in 2009. After the post-crisis peak in 2011, exports have been moving slowly since 2012. Although there was a decent expansion in 2013 and 2014, the export growth rate dwindled and became negative in 2015 and 2016. Unlike the previous crises in 1997 and 2001, exports were not recovered in the subsequent years after the GFC. Instead, exports growth rates have remained stagnant for five consecutive years between 2011 and 2016.

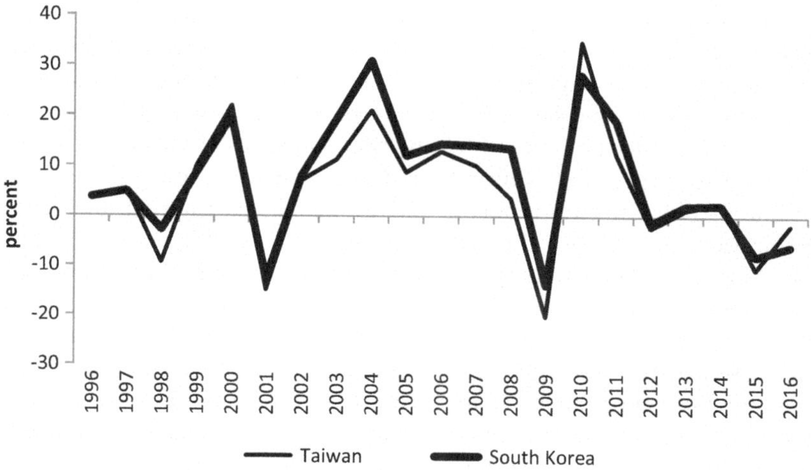

Fig. 4.1 Annual export growth rates in Taiwan and South Korea 1996–2016. Source: Bureau of Foreign Trade, Taiwan; KOSIS

Feeble demand from Western countries for final consumption goods partially explains the weak exports. In fact, the slow growth in exports could be a signal of the manufacturing sector's decreasing competitiveness. As Taiwan and South Korea have been relying on exporting intermediate goods to developing countries, the slowing down of exports implies that their role as "middle-technology providers" is waning. Although Taiwan's and South Korea's productivity have increased over the last two decades, this progress is not sufficient to maintain a technology lead over emerging competitors. At the same time, the developing countries, in particular China, have been actively upgrading their domestic industries and exporting goods with higher technology and capital intensity. The so-called red-supply chain, the fast-growing cluster of high-tech companies cultivated by the Chinese government, has set many Chinese manufacturers in direct competition with Taiwanese and Korean counterparts in a variety of manufacturing products. Taiwan is competing with Chinese counterparts in LCD flat panels as well as LED lighting and electronic components for mobile phones. Beyond the direct trade competition in high-technology products, the Taiwanese government is also concerned about technology transfer to China through Chinese companies' acquisitions of Taiwanese firms in recent years.

For Korea, the growing competition from China is also a serious concern. According to a report by the Korea Evaluation Institute of Industrial Technology, the average gap with China in 24 key industries including biotechnology and displays is 0.9 years. Chinese and Korean technology in high-end smartphones, wearables, memory chips, and smart electronics is expected to nearly commensurate within the next five years (The STAR Online 2017). Another report issued by the Korea International Trade Association in 2015 also showed the growing competition from China in the US market. The competition is especially severe in mobile phones and components, shipbuilding, and electrical and electronic products. The market share of Chinese products in the US strengthened particularly in the plastic plates and lighting equipment parts sectors whereas market share for Korean products fell in those areas. Korea's market share in telephone sets for cellular networks decreased to the 10 percent range while China's market share has reached 80 percent (KITA 2015).

China's industrial catchup can be seen from its greater share in exports of global intermediate goods. According to the WTO statistics, China was the second largest global exporter and importer of intermediate goods in 2014, after the EU. Its share in world exports of intermediate goods increased from 5.6 percent in 2004 to 12.0 percent in 2014. In comparison, Taiwan's share progressed only slightly from 2.3 percent to 2.8 percent. South Korea's share also enlarged rather insignificantly from 2.9 percent to 3.3 percent during the same period (WTO 2016). China's increasing importance in producing intermediate goods has corroded the global market shares of Taiwanese and Korean manufacturers. Maintaining a technological edge over China is the only solution to make their products more competitive. However, with lack of industrial upgrading, level of technology cannot be improved, which implies worsening profitability for companies and in turn wage stagnation for domestic workers. Eventually, private domestic consumption could be depressed as a consequence.

Overview of Taiwan's Industrial Upgrading Policies

In 2002, Taiwan's Ministry of Economic Affairs (MOEA) initiated the "Two Trillion and Twin Star Development Program" with the aim to help Taiwan's high-technology sectors reach another milestone. The "two trillion industries" refer to the semiconductor and color-imaging industries which were each expected to generate over one trillion in production value (in New Taiwan dollars). In particular, the flat panel was the main sector for development in the color-imaging industry. The "twin star industries" refer to the digital content (including software, media, online games, music, publishing, etc.) and biotechnology industries. The "twin star industries" were considered to be potential leading industries in the future. In addition to having a tax credit scheme for developing these industries, the Southern Taiwan Science Park and Central Taiwan Science Park were also developed into two new clusters for the IC and LCD subsectors. As a result of promotion through this program, the major components within the semiconductor industries, such as IC foundry, IC packaging, and IC design were quickly developed. Taiwan's global share in producing components for semiconductor and color-imaging industries increased quickly in the early 2000s. Taiwan thus became a global leading producer for LCD monitors, optical discs, IC foundry, and IC packaging and testing. Despite the initial success, the major subsectors involved in "Two Trillion and Twin Star Development Program" became hot potatoes for the government in the subsequent years due to the huge loss in profits. The lack of "core technology" is a main cause for the shrinking shares in global market and declining profits. For example, the dynamic random-access memory (DRAM) sector once accounted for 23.3 percent of global market share in 2008. The ratio declined quickly to only 6.3 percent in 2011. The government helped with initial financial capital injection for DRAM development. However, most of the DRAM companies looked for short-term profitability, instead of investing in R&D for long-term development. The continuous huge payment for purchasing foreign high technology diminished profit margins of Taiwanese companies. Policy inconsistency is another reason as the Ma Ying-jeou government (2008–2016) did not continue to support the "Two Trillion and Twin Star Development Program" initiated during the previous Chen Shui-bian government (2000–2008). Some DPP politicians even griped that the exclusion of flat panels in the early harvest program under ECFA allowed China to develop the flat panel sector quickly and usurp Taiwan's leading position in the global market.

Apart from nurturing ICT sector development in the early 2000s, the government had also concurrently promoted development of the services sector. The government had considered that it was too *risky* for *Taiwan's economy* to rely heavily on ICT production alone. Taiwan's economy would severely suffer if global demand for ICT products began to diminish. Therefore, a policy that aimed at diversifying industrial development became imperative. In 2004, the Taiwanese government began to incorporate the services sector into the national development plan, with the objective that both the manufacturing and services sectors could be the two engines of Taiwan's economic development. "Taiwan's Service Industry Development Plan" was approved by the Executive Yuan in 2009. Six services subsectors, namely tourism, healthcare, cultural creativity, high-end agriculture, green energy, and biotechnology, were prioritized for development and they became known as the six key emerging industries. In October 2009, ten key service industries were selected as major industries for promotion. This plan was carried out from 2009 to 2012. Each of the government agencies concerned was expected to map out and execute concrete action plans in accordance with the strategies and measures set out in this plan. In 2010, four key intelligent industries were proposed to complement the six key emerging industries and ten key service industries, namely the "Double 10 Flagship Plan", to pave the way for long-term industrial development in Taiwan (Table 4.2). However, the implementation of this industrial development plan did not significantly improve the share of services in the economy and the ICT industry still accounted for a large share in Taiwan's economy. In fact, some of the industries selected do not possess any significance to Taiwan's

Table 4.2 Taiwan's Industrial Development Plan 2004–2009

Double ten flagship plan		
Ten flagship plans	*Ten flagship plans*	
Ten *Key industries*	*Six* *Key emerging industries*	*Four* *Emerging smart industries*
1. International medical care 2. International logistics 3. Music and digital content 4. Conventions and exhibitions 5. Urban renewal 6. WiMAX 7. Chinese e-commerce 8. Education 9. Finance 10. Internationalization of cuisines	1. Agriculture with high quality 2. Culture and creativity 3. Tourism and travel 4. Medicine and healthcare 5. Green energy 6. Biotechnology	1. Cloud computing 2. Green architectures 3. Electric vehicles 4. Industrial patents and inventions

Source: CEPD (2017)

economy, such as "international cuisine", "Chinese e-Commerce", "high-quality agriculture", and "culture and creativity". Indeed, the selected industries functioned more like a slogan rather than actually contributing to industrial upgrading or to Taiwan's economic progress.

Since 2011, the government has lowered corporate income tax from 25 percent to 17 percent. Taiwan has for a long time granted certain tax incentives to industrial and high-tech subsectors, but not often granted benefits to the services sector. The significance of slashing the tax rate to 17 percent, applying to both the industrial and services sectors, signified that the Taiwanese government attached equal importance to future development of the two sectors. Moreover, Ma's administration also believed that improved cross-Strait economic relations would offer Taiwanese entrepreneurs a great and growing market to accrue potential commercial profits in China's services sector (Focus Taiwan News Channel 2010).

Like the Ma government, the current Tsai administration also considers Taiwan as being overdependent on the ICT industry. Initiatives have thus geared toward increasing the competitiveness of other manufacturing industries through industrial upgrading policies. The priority industries for development are green technology, the Internet of Things, biotechnology, precision machinery, and defense. These five industries were selected to be developed in various industrial clusters in Taiwan. The government intends to encourage integration among foreign investment, academic research, and industry in the selected industrial clusters. Tsai also planned to set up a "quasi-sovereign fund" to help develop the target industries. The Tsai administration aims to facilitate greater business opportunities for local manufacturers by enhancing industrial cooperation with advanced countries. For instance, the government plans to attract Silicon Valley entrepreneurs to invest in Taiwan's manufacturing sector, to enhance Taiwan's innovation capability and supply chain linkage with the US. Diaspora ties may also help. Taiwanese Americans and Taiwanese expatriates are prominent in the US technology sector (among them Jerry Yang, co-founder of Yahoo, and Steve Chen, co-founder of YouTube).

Industrial upgrading needs long-term investment in R&D, but it is questionable whether the government can ensure the long-term commitment given the short-term pressures on many politicians for elections. If the economy fails to pick up within a few years, politicians will be pressed to respond with policy changes, even to policies that might eventually have yielded results. More sustainable industrial cooperation with advanced countries will be realized only when Taiwan can improve its judicial system's transparency, efficiency, and independence, especially on intellectual property rights. In the meantime, excluding China from Taiwan's industrial development is unrealistic. Attracted by short-term profit, more Taiwanese manufacturing firms are likely to opt to cooperate with Chinese counterparts. Tsai's government will have to accommodate this market-driven cross-Strait integration in manufacturing while trying to maintain Taiwan's technology superiority. In fact, some selected industries and policy measures overlap with those of the Ma administration. There is also similarity in the underlying principle of targeting industries for support rather than focusing on creating a business-friendly environment and trusting that market forces will determine the most competitive sectors.

Overview of South Korea's Main Industrial Upgrading Policies

South Korea's public R&D program traditionally targeted large-scale industrial technology developed by chaebols. After the AFC, the South Korean government sought to shift S&T policy toward supporting more fundamental research, with less emphasis on technology development by chaebols. Therefore, attention has been increasingly paid to issues such as commercialization of R&D, financing for innovative firms, and development of innovation intermediaries (OECD 2009).

The Five-Year Plan for Science and Technology Innovation was launched in December 1997 with an aim to promote the national R&D capacity to the level of G-7 countries. In 1999, the Korean government organized a committee to formulate "Vision 2025: Korea's Long-Term Plan for Scientific and Technological Development" to reinforce the country's innovation capability. The plan has several features, including the shift of innovation system from government-led to private-sector-led, improvement of the effectiveness of national R&D investment and aligning the R&D system from a domestic to a global network. To turn the vision into reality by the year of 2025, the Korean government launched the 21st Century Frontier Science Program in 1999 and enacted the Science and Technology Framework Law. Under the law, two five-year Science and Technology Principal Plans (2003–2007 and 2008–2012) were formulated. Several policy measures have been launched to promote the national innovation system and to strengthen the innovation capacity of private sectors. Known as "577 initiative", the plan under Lee Myung-Bak set several ambitious targets: to reach an R&D intensity of 5 percent by 2012, from 3.2 percent in 2006, to focus on seven areas of R&D and to become an important S&T power in the world (OECD 2009). Ninety strategic technologies with the potential for considerable impact on Korea's economic growth were identified. Thirty-three technologies were selected as national strategic technologies (Table 4.3). The "577 initiative" further identified 50 critical technologies and 40 candidate technologies in several major technology areas. The third Science and Technology (S&T) Basic Plan (2013–2017) sets out the government's roadmap for economic

Table 4.3 South Korea's thirty-three priority technologies

Category	*Technology*
Information technology and electronics	Next-generation network technology, mobile internet, and 4G mobile communications technology, USN technology, information protection technology, next-generation system S/W technology
Bioscience and biotechnology	Stem cell application technology, preclinical/clinical technology for new drug development, new drug target and new drug candidate development technology, drug delivery technology, high-value-added processing and production technology of agricultural, marine, and livestock products, technology for early diagnosis of cancer, safety, and risk assessment technology
Machinery and manufacturing process	Intelligent service robot technology, environmentally friendly automobile technology, ultra-precision processing and device technology, Intelligent production system technology (machinery, processing, textiles, etc.)
Energy and resources	Hydrogen energy production and storage technology, next-generation cell (secondary cell, fuel cell) technology, new and renewable technologies, highly efficient energy use technology
Space, aviation, and marine	Satellite (body, payload) development technology, marine technology, marine environment investigation and conservation, and management technology
Environment	Environmentally friendly production and processing technology, air pollution reduction and treatment technology, resource recycling and safe waste treatment technology, environment preservation and restoration technology, technology to mitigate and respond to natural disasters
Materials and nano	Photon and electron fusion materials, nano-level material processing technology
Construction, transport, and safety	Technology to create high-speed trains with a max speed of 400km/h, state-of-the-art light rail transit and urban-type magnetic levitation train technology, high-tech logistics technology

Source: OECD (2009)

development by seeking diversification of the national economy toward wider range of sectors and technologies (OECD 2015).

Like Taiwan, the South Korean government has also sought to promote services sector development by integrating both the services and manufacturing sectors. The importance of promoting high-value-added services was recognized as early as during the Lee Myung-bak administration (2008–2013). Despite their greater contribution to domestic employment, most of Korea's services are low-value-added. Integrating services and manufacturing is therefore considered essential to help enhance services sector competitiveness. Another way to promote services sector development is through deregulation to boost business competition. A lot of government restrictions on the services sector aimed at protecting employment in SMEs. However, there is a serious risk that they may end up stifling the growth and dynamism of the sector (Park and Shin 2012). When the manufacturing sector suffers from global economic recession, the services sector must be resilient to sustain economic growth. A competitive and high-value-added services sector is also essential to attract young talents. In 2015, the Korean government identified seven potential services for development, including healthcare, tourism, financial services, education, logistics, and software services (Table 4.4). Several rules and measures were amended to meet the development needs of these services (Su 2016).

While the government spent much effort on drafting a vision for Korea's future industrial and technology development, chaebols have continued to act as a key player in Korea's R&D spending. Over the past few decades, South Korean companies have moved from safe technology investments and incremental innovation toward cutting-edge science-based innovation. Today, technology innovation in the South Korean economy is primarily driven by large manufacturing giants such as Samsung, Hyundai, Pohang Iron and Steel Company (POSCO), and LG Electronics. As mentioned in Chap. 3, President Park Geun-hye announced plans in 2013 to build a "Creative Economy" which aims to promote a new growth model based on innovation and entrepreneurship. Nonetheless, such "innovation-driven" economic growth serves only to enhance the country's reliance on chaebols which accounted for most of the private R&D investments. While the chaebol is important in South Korea's technology advancement, it is often criticized for its non-transparent culture and many of its business practices are considered corrupt. Moreover, the growth of the chaebol has come at the expense of SMEs, thus creating a dichotomous economy.

Table 4.4 Seven targeted service sectors for development in South Korea

Sectors	*Development strategies*
Healthcare	• Promote IT-medical service convergence • Ease regulations to improve consumer convenience • Increase the number of over-the-counter medications • Develop a mobile app-based healthcare system • Promote medical tourism and medical equipment manufacturing
Tourism	• Develop target market specific tourism programs • Ease environment regulations to grow cruise and mountain sports industries • Increase tourist accommodations and tourist information centers • Develop tourism workforce
Contents	• Strengthen intellectual property rights • Give up to 10 percent tax deduction for audiovisual content creation • Extend content property-based loans • Increase investment in content development
Education	• Promote the use of high technology in education • Ease regulations regarding the management of foreign school branches in Korea
Financial services	• Innovate financial services through ICT-financial service convergence • Develop a variety of financial services • Transform the Korea Exchange into a holding company
Software	• Promote the use of cloud computing (e.g., revise regulations on information security, such as requirements to use separate servers and networks)
Logistics	• Work on developing markets for high-tech logistics services • Develop the freight delivery market

Source: Ministry of Strategy and Finance (2017)

Chaebols' dominance in the economy could also create obstacles for new entrepreneurs' entry into the market and depress the prospects of a venture-backed, start-up culture (Gupta et al. 2013).

Changes in export commodities

Industrial upgrading is a process by which a country can move up the global value chain and produce more value-added products. To maintain their roles as "middle-technology providers" in the hierarchy of the global production network, both countries have been making effort to upgrade their domestic industries. The results of their industrial upgrading efforts can be seen from the changes in major export items.

Over the past two decades, both Taiwan and Korean exports have been shifting from manufactured goods to commodities with higher technology and capital intensity. Taiwan's official statistics showed that its exports with high degree of technology and capital intensity have significantly improved over the last two decades (Council for Economic Planning and Development 2017). Similarly, the data from the World Bank also showed that Korea's export of high-technology goods increased from US$29.8 billion in 1995 to US$126.5 billion in 2015 (World Bank 2017). Although both governments also tried to diversify the exports of industrial goods, the export structure shows that both countries have been inclining toward production of ICT goods. Table 4.5 shows Taiwan's exports by items from 2001 to 2016. Over the last 15 years, Taiwan has increasingly concentrated on exporting chemical products and electrical machinery. The shares of chemical products in Taiwan's total exports grew from 9.8 percent in 2001 to around 20 percent during the 2008–2014 period and declined to 15.9 percent in 2016. The export share of electrical machinery also developed clearly from 21.6 percent in 2001 to 36.2 percent in 2016.

Table 4.5 Taiwan's exports by items 2001–2016

	Agriculture and food stuffs	*Chemical products*	*Manufactured goods*	*Capital equipment*		*Others*
				Electrical machinery	*Other capital equipment*	
2001	1.4	9.8	19.2	21.6	35.7	12.3
2002	1.3	10.5	18.7	22.9	34.7	11.9
2003	1.3	11.7	17.9	24.1	31.7	13.3
2004	1.2	13.4	17.6	26.0	28.0	13.8
2005	1.1	16.0	17.1	26.3	25.1	14.4
2006	0.9	16.2	16.8	29.0	22.1	15.0
2007	0.8	18.5	16.9	29.0	20.2	14.6
2008	1.0	20.9	16.5	27.5	19.3	14.8
2009	1.1	19.5	15.6	30.0	18.9	14.9
2010	1.0	19.4	15.0	29.8	19.7	15.1
2011	1.1	20.3	15.7	27.9	20.7	14.3
2012	1.3	21.1	15.4	28.5	19.9	13.8
2013	1.3	21.7	14.6	30.0	19.1	13.3
2014	1.3	20.1	14.6	32.1	18.9	13.0
2015	1.4	16.7	14.4	34.0	20.9	12.6
2016	1.4	15.9	13.9	36.2	20.7	11.9

Source: Ministry of Finance (Taiwan)
Unit: As percent of total exports

During the same period, the export share of manufactured goods declined from 19.2 percent to 13.9 percent. A similar development can be found in South Korea (Table 4.6). Chemical products and electrical machinery have taken a greater share in Korea's exports while the share of manufactured goods has been declining. Overall, integrated circuits, essential components for making ICT goods, accounted for a significant share in Taiwan's and South Korea's exports of electrical machinery. In other words, while both Taiwan and Korea have been promoting industrial development across different sectors, ICT-related products and chemical goods are still the driving forces behind their export growth. The industrial upgrading appears to have only taken off in a particular industry. A possible reason may be the governments' long-term commitment to develop the electronics industry since the 1980s while the promotion of other industries began only in recent years.

The greater exports of high-value-added products do not necessarily mean a success in industrial upgrading. Indeed, the lack of advanced technology has resulted in a particular pattern of upgrading for the latecomers

Table 4.6 South Korea's exports by items 2001–2016

	Agriculture and food stuffs	*Chemical products*	*Manufactured goods*	*Capital equipment*		*Others*
				Electrical machinery	*Other capital equipment*	
2001	1.7	14.7	17.8	14.4	43.2	8.2
2002	1.5	13.5	16.6	14.6	46.7	7.0
2003	1.4	13.3	15.5	14.8	47.7	7.3
2004	1.2	14.2	14.6	14.4	48.6	7.0
2005	1.1	16.3	14.4	15.1	45.9	7.2
2006	0.9	17.2	14.3	14.9	44.2	8.5
2007	0.9	17.9	14.0	13.7	44.6	8.9
2008	0.9	20.4	14.1	11.7	43.7	9.1
2009	1.1	17.9	13.2	13.1	43.7	10.9
2010	1.1	18.7	13.0	15.1	41.5	10.7
2011	1.1	22.0	13.8	14.0	40.1	9.0
2012	1.2	23.0	13.8	15.6	36.9	9.4
2013	1.1	22.7	12.8	17.3	37.3	8.8
2014	1.1	22.1	13.2	17.1	38.0	8.6
2015	1.2	18.5	12.8	18.4	40.6	8.6
2016	1.4	17.1	12.8	17.6	38.5	12.6

Source: KOSIS

(Chu 2015) such as Taiwan and Korea. Due to comparative technological backwardness, many Taiwanese and Korean firms relied on importing capital equipment and key components from abroad to produce high-value-added products. Hence, the increase in imports of capital investment is often an indication of growing exports and economic growth in the following months. Capital investment is also one of the components of economic growth. The government's investment in infrastructure and private sectors' investment in plant and equipment would fuel higher economic growth rates. However, as private sectors' capital investment reduces their profits, Taiwan companies' low-profit margin based on OEM production often discourages local manufacturers to make capital investment. On the other hand, Korea chaebols with greater financial resources are able to invest in high-technology equipment and produce high-value-added goods. The scale economies are thus essential for large firms to increase production efficiency and maintain their profit margin. The higher return, through exporting higher value-added goods, allows large firms to invest more in R&D to advance their level of technology furthermore.

Strong Reliance on Foreign Technology Despite the Large R&D Spending

In line with the industrial development policy aimed at innovation and technology advancement, Taiwan's and Korea's R&D spending has been increasing. R&D expenditure as a percentage of GDP in Taiwan has clearly enlarged from 1.91 percent in 1998 to 3 percent in 2014. In South Korea, the growth in R&D expenditure is even greater. Korea's R&D expenditure as percentage of GDP grew from 2.34 percent to 4.29 percent during the same period (Table 4.7). By international standards, the R&D expenditure as percentage of GDP in Taiwan and South Korea are comparable to that in most advanced countries. For example, in 2014, the R&D expenditure as percentage of GDP in Germany was 2.85 percent, 2.23 percent in France, 3.59 percent in Japan, and 2.72 in the US in 2013 (Ministry of Science and Technology 2016). However, due to Taiwan's smaller economic size, its R&D expenditure in absolute terms is relatively insignificant. In 2014, Taiwan's R&D expenditure was US$32,440 million whereas South Korea's is US$72,267 million. Seventy-nine percent of Taiwan's R&D expenditure came from the private sector. The ratio for South Korea was 77 percent according to the official statistics.

Table 4.7 The R&D expenditure as a percentage of GDP in Taiwan and South Korea 1998–2014

	Taiwan	*South Korea*
1998	1.91	2.34
1999	1.98	2.25
2000	1.97	2.39
2001	2.08	2.59
2002	2.18	2.53
2003	2.31	2.63
2004	2.38	2.85
2005	2.45	2.98
2006	2.58	3.23
2007	2.62	3.00
2008	2.68	3.12
2009	2.84	3.29
2010	2.80	3.47
2011	2.90	3.74
2012	2.95	4.03
2013	3.00	4.15
2014	3.00	4.29

Source: National Development Council (2016), Science & Technology Policy Research and Information Center (2012)

Although Taiwan has made progress in R&D expenditure, there is still much room for improvement. Recent years have seen a return of overseas Taiwanese financial capital, but the business environment was such that significant amounts of this "idle capital" went into property or the stock market rather than industry. According to official estimates, there was by 2013 at least NT$10 trillion of "idle capital" in Taiwan's financial market (CNA News 2013). The question of how to convert "idle capital", generated mostly from rich entrepreneurs, from speculative investment to "real investment" in industrial upgrading and technology advancement is critical for Taiwan's economic advancement. Unlike Taiwanese companies' lack of resources for innovation due to the smaller profit margins, Korean chaebols might have greater financial resources for R&D investment. Nonetheless, there is a concern that the family-ownership management style might lead chaebol leaders to pursue short-term personal benefits, instead of the companies' long-term development needs.

The large R&D investment has not significantly changed Taiwan's and South Korea's technology dependence on the advanced countries. This technology dependence can be seen from the technology balance of payments. According to the OECD, "technology balance of payments registers the commercial transactions related to international technology and know-how transfers" (OECD 2006). To evaluate the technology dependence, the technology balance of payments ratio, which refers to the amounts of money used to purchase foreign technology divided by technology sold to other countries, is employed. A greater ratio means more technology is sold to other countries than purchased from other countries. Therefore, larger ratios indicate lesser dependence on foreign technology. In 2014, Taiwan's technology balance of payments ratio (technology product receipts/money paid for using technology products) was 0.21, less than that of 0.25 in 2009 (Table 4.8). In comparison, South Korea had progressed from 0.42 in 2009 to 0.57 in 2013. Compared with most of the advanced countries, the technology balance of payment ratios in Taiwan and Korea are relatively low and that shows their greater dependence on technology from abroad. In 2014, Japan's ratio was 7.13, the US' was 1.52, Germany's 1.31, and UK's 2.35 (Ministry of Science and Technology 2016). According to official figures, Taiwan's high-technology imports mainly come from the US, accounting for 76 percent of Taiwan's total technology imports in 2013, followed by 16 percent from Japan. Likewise, Japan and the US are also Korea's traditional sources of high technology.

Another indicator for the technology dependence is the royalties and license fees in service trade. Both Taiwan and South Korea have run up a large amount of service trade deficit in this service item. In 2013, Taiwan had a US$3532 million trade deficit in royalties and license fees and South Korea had US$5409 million of deficit in royalties and license fees (UNCTAD statistics). Korea's greater deficit does not mean it is more dependent on foreign technology than Taiwan. In fact, Korea has exported

Table 4.8 Coverage ratio of technology balance of payments in Taiwan and South Korea 2009–2014

	Taiwan	*South Korea*
2009	0.25	0.42
2010	0.18	0.33
2011	n/a	0.41
2012	0.18	0.48
2013	0.20	0.57
2014	0.21	n/a

Source: Ministry of Science and Technology (2016)

more royalties and license fees (US$4107 million) than Taiwan (US$1017 million) in 2013. However, it had greater imports of royalties and license fees (US$9598 million), thus amounting to its larger total deficit.

Conclusion

The main conclusion from the previous analysis is summarized as follows. First, after the relocation of labor-intensive manufacturing production to overseas countries, Taiwan and South Korea have turned to depend on exporting intermediate goods to developing countries, mostly China, for the final assembly. Nonetheless, the slow progress of industrial upgrading at home and quick industrial catchup in China is one of the causes for the waning exports of intermediate goods in recent years.

Second, Taiwan's R&D expenditure is lagging behind South Korea's. Taiwanese manufacturers' long-term reliance on OEM, which emphasizes on cost-saving instead of innovation, made their profit margins small. The small profit limited their ability to invest in R&D, which in turn prevents them from upgrading to higher margin production. In addition, the slow progress of industrial upgrading also restrained the growth in wages. The less attractive salary limited the possibility of employing national and international talents in services or high-value-added sectors. The relatively low salary explained the outflow of Taiwanese talents in high-value-added sectors to overseas countries. Successful industrial upgrading requires not only sufficient investment in capital equipment and in high technology but also skillful labors.

Third, Taiwan and South Korea began to concentrate on producing chemical goods and key components in making ICT products. However, the high volume of exports in the capital- and technology-intensive goods does not necessarily mean there is fundamental change to technological capabilities. Despite the improvement in R&D expenditure in the past few years, both countries still relied on high technology imported from other advanced countries.

Finally, Taiwan and South Korea are two typical countries that actively pursued industrial upgrading in order to maintain export competitiveness. One difference is that Korea has moved ahead of Taiwan in making branded ICT products. In comparison, many firms in Taiwan do not pursue R&D-intensive and own-brand strategies to catch up. They continued to rely on OEM with low-profit margin. The Korean government's national champion policy and long-term commitment to chaebols has produced some successful global brands.

References

Campbell, Joel R. (2012). Building an IT economy: South Korea science and technology policy. Center for technology innovation at Brookings. Retrieved October 23, 2017, from https://www.brookings.edu/wp-content/uploads/2016/06/CTI_19-_Korea_Tech_Paper_Formatted.pdf

Chu, W.-w. (2015). Latecomer upgrading in Taiwan. *Journal of the Asia-Pacific Economy, 20*(3), 369–384.

CNA News. (2013, December 7). Interest rate is the key for the potential fall of housing prices. Retrieved December 11, 2013, from http://www.cna.com.tw/news/afe/201312070149-1.aspx (in Chinese).

Council for Economic Planning and Development (CEPD, Taiwan). (2017). Taiwan's Industrial Development Policy (tai wan chan ye fa zhan zheng ce). Retrieved March 1, 2018, from https://www.ndc.gov.tw/Content_List.aspx?n=80BC9D0DD7FF1FBB

Focus Taiwan News Channel (2010, March 30). Taiwan approves record amount of investment in China in 2010. Retrieved April 1, 2011, from http://focustaiwan.tw/ShowNews/WebNews_Detail.aspx?ID=201103300039&Type=aECO

Gupta, N., Healey, D. W., & Shipp, S. S. (2013, August). Innovation policies of South Korea. Institute for Defense Analyses. Retrieved October 23, 2017, from https://www.ida.org/idamedia/Corporate/Files/Publications/STPIPubs/ida-d-4984.ashx

Korea International Trade Association (KITA). (2015, July 3). Export Competition between Korea and Japan is Getting Fiercer in the U.S. Import Market. Retrieved May 8, 2017, from http://www.kita.org/about/iitView.do?id=&no=1811&searchWrd=&pageIndex=1

Ministry of Science and Technology (Taiwan). (2016, December 5). *Taiwan's scientific technology development and prospect.* The tenth National Science and Technology Conference. Retrieved May 8, 2017, from https://www.most.gov.tw/tc/10th/images/present.pdf

Ministry of Strategy and Finance (ROK). (2017). *Service sector development plan.* Retrieved May 4, 2017, from https://english.mosf.go.kr/

National Development Council (Taiwan). (2002). *Taiwan Statistical Data Book 2002.* Taipei: Executive Yuan (Taiwan).

National Development Council (Taiwan). (2016). *Taiwan Statistical Data Book 2016.* Taipei: Executive Yuan (Taiwan).

National Statistics (Taiwan). (2017). Retrieved April 12, 2017, from http://www.stat.gov.tw/mp.asp?mp=4

OECD. (2006). Glossary of statistical terms. Retrieved May 8, 2017, from https://stats.oecd.org/glossary/detail.asp?ID=2693

OECD. (2009). *OECD review of innovation policy: Korea.* Paris: OECD Publishing.

OECD. (2015, October). Korea: Policy priorities for a dynamic, inclusive and creative economy. Retrieved May 3, 2017, from https://www.oecd.org/korea/korea-policy-priorities-for-a-dynamic-inclusive-and-creative-economy-EN.pdf

Park, D., & Shin, K. (2012). Performance of the Service Sector in the Republic of Korea: An Empirical Investigation. ADB Economics Working Paper Series, No. 324. Retrieved October 23, 2017, from https://www.adb.org/sites/default/files/publication/30081/economics-wp324.pdf

Science & Technology Policy Research and Information Center (Taiwan). (2012). *Yearbook of Science and Technology (zhong hua min guo ke xue ji shu nian jian).* Taipei: Science & Technology Policy Research and Information Center.

Su, Y-W. (2016). South Korea's government's policy measure to promote potential service sectors (han guo zheng fu ji ji fa zhan qian li fu wu ye zhi zuo fa). WTO Paper 493. Retrieved October 23, 2017, from http://web.wtocenter.org.tw/Page.aspx?nid=126&pid=275507

The STAR Online. (2017, April 5). South Korea's high-tech economy threatened by Chinese catch-up. Retrieved May 7, 2017, from http://www.thestar.com.my/tech/tech-news/2017/04/05/south-koreas-high-tech-economy-threatened-by-chinese-catch-up/

The World Bank. (2017). World Bank Open Data. Retrieved May 8, 2017, from http://data.worldbank.org/indicator/TX.VAL.TECH.CD?page=1

United Nations Conference on Trade and Development (UNCTAD). Retrieved May 8, 2017., from http://unctadstat.unctad.org/EN/Index.html

World Trade Organization. (2016). *World Trade Statistical Review 2016.* Retrieved May 4, 2017, from https://www.wto.org/english/res_e/statis_e/wts2016_e/wts16_toc_e.htm

CHAPTER 5

Comparing Governments' Policies in Promoting the Economic Growth (II): Free Trade Policy

Abstract Taiwan and South Korean governments have tried to further economic liberalization through both bilateral and multilateral FTAs. Due to the political pressure from China, the development of Taiwan's FTA network is progressing slowly. In comparison, South Korea has successfully extended its FTA links with various important economies in the world. Although South Korea's trade surplus in goods has been gradually developed, its service trade deficit has enlarged. This indicates that South Korea's greater involvement in the global economy through FTAs has strengthened its comparative advantage in manufacturing production while the services sector did not benefit from the greater economic opening up. Unlike South Korea, Taiwan's overall trade in goods and services has been relatively unchanged in the last two decades.

Keywords Free trade agreement (FTA) • Regional comprehensive economic partnership (RCEP) • Trans-Pacific Partnership (TPP) • Economic Cooperation Framework Agreement (ECFA) • South Korea-US Free Trade Agreement (KORUS)

To promote the export-oriented economic development, Taiwan and South Korea encouraged exports and maintained relatively high tariffs for imports in the 1960s and 1970s. Partly in response to the US trade protectionism, both Taiwan and South Korea began to lower import tariff

M.-H. Chiang, *Post-Industrial Development in East Asia*,
https://doi.org/10.1007/978-981-13-0274-9_5

rates and liberalize their external trade regulations since the 1980s. The nominal import tariff in Taiwan was reduced by a wide margin, from 31 percent in 1983 to 13 percent in 1988 (Cheung et al. 1997). By 2001, its average nominal tariff rate had fallen to 8.2 percent (Dent 2002). Similarly, South Korea began to reduce its import tariff since the 1980s. The greater commitment to international trade rules and principles during the Uruguay Round of GATT in 1994 further encouraged the country to phase in agreed tariff reduction and other non-tariff barriers. The country significantly accelerated its trade liberalization process after the AFC. The Kim Dae-jung government's new trade policy aimed at transforming South Korea into an "open trading nation". By 2000, the average tariff rate in Korea had declined to only 7.5 percent (Dent 2002).

After the 2000s, FTA became the main driving force behind Taiwan's and South Korea's trade liberalization. Both governments believed that FTA would not only benefit exports but also improve the competitiveness of their domestic sectors. Both countries initially embraced multilateral FTAs and, later on, bilateral FTA. South Korea had joined the WTO since its establishment as early as in 1995. Taiwan formally became a member of the WTO in 2002. The stagnation of the Doha round trade negotiations was a setback for the development of multilateral FTA. However, it has given a fresh impetus for both countries to move toward bilateral trade negotiations. Political pressure from China has been an important factor in explaining Taiwan's slow progress in the development of its bilateral FTAs. On the other hand, South Korea's FTAs have been developing relatively smoothly over the last two decades.

The purpose of this chapter is to compare the evolution of FTA policy in Taiwan and South Korea and the consequences on their overall trade development over the last two decades. The first section examines Taiwan's FTA strategy. Given the political pressure from China, Taiwan has shifted its strategy by initiating bilateral economic agreements with other countries in selected issues or sectors. Taiwan under the Ma Ying-jeou administration sought to expand Taiwan's FTA network by establishing good relations with China first. The Tsai Ing-wen government however had adopted another strategy, hoping to diversify Taiwan's economic reliance from China to other countries. In the second section, the evolution of South Korea's FTA policy is discussed. Unlike Taiwan, South Korea does not have diplomatic constraints when developing its institutionalized economic ties with other countries. The Korean governments since the Kim administration have been pursuing an FTA expansion policy. The administrations after Kim have followed suit. In the third and fourth sections, Taiwan's and South Korea's trade development in the last two decades is compared. Although South Korea's merchandise trade surplus has been improving over the last few years, its service trade deficit has been worsening. In comparison, Taiwan's trade in goods and services has changed relatively little. The more extensive FTAs seem to have strengthened Korea's comparative advantage in manufacturing while the less competitive services sector suffered from the growing foreign competition. The conclusion summarizes the important points and future trade development prospects of the two countries.

Taiwan's FTA Strategy: FTAs as Diplomatic Breakthrough

Several bilateral and multilateral FTAs have been quickly signed in the Asia-Pacific region in recent decades. To avoid marginalization in the wave of economic regionalism, Taiwan has actively sought to establish FTAs with other countries. However, due to China's objection, the prospects of several FTA projects by Taiwan were diminished. The Chinese government expressed its opposition to its diplomatic partners which expressed interest to sign FTAs with Taiwan, warning potential political troubles and adverse effect on economic relations with China (Dent 2006). As China becomes more and more dominant in the regional political economy, other countries clearly understand the political and economic benefits of maintaining good relations with China. Still, Taiwan managed to implement FTAs with Panama in 2004, Guatemala in 2006, and Nicaragua, Salvador, and Honduras in 2008. In 2013, Taiwan signed economic agreements with New Zealand and Singapore respectively (Table 5.1). Indeed, the FTAs with the above countries are more politically symbolic than economically substantive. The above countries accounted for a small portion of Taiwan's external trade. Apparently, signing FTAs with these small countries is not in Taiwan's economic interests. The five Latin American countries that implemented FTAs with Taiwan all have diplomatic relations with the island. The FTAs with them signified a cement of diplomatic relations. As ASEAN is an ideal alternative market for Taiwan's exports of industrial goods and an investment destination other than China, the ANZTEC with New Zealand and ASTEP with Singapore are important milestones for Taiwan to initiate trade talks with ASEAN in the future.

Table 5.1 Taiwan's economic agreements with other countries

	Type of agreement	*Date of signing*	*Implementation date*	*As % of Taiwan's exports in 2016*	*As % of Taiwan's imports in 2016*
Panama	FTA	21 August 2003	1 January 2004	0.05	0.01
Guatemala	FTA	22 September 2005	1 July 2006	0.04	0.03
Nicaragua	FTA	16 June 2006	1 January 2008	0.01	0.04
El Salvador	FTA	7 May 2007	1 March 2008	0.04	0.02
Honduras	FTA	7 May 2007	15 July 2008	0.03	0.02
China	Economic cooperation framework agreement	29 June 2010	1 January 2011	26.2	19.1
Singapore	Economic partnership	7 November 2013	19 April 2014	5.9	3.3
New Zealand	Economic cooperation	10 July 2013	1 December 2013	0.2	0.4
Total	n/a			32.47	22.92

Source: Bureau of Foreign Trade (2017)

The Taiwanese government's view has been that its economy would suffer from being excluded in the institutionalized regional economic integration, especially when its main competitor, South Korea, has been ahead of Taiwan in extending the FTA network. The Ma administration believed that political reconciliation with China could allow Taiwan to make a breakthrough in establishing FTAs with other economies. Given China's growing influence in the region, broader cross-strait economic integration was regarded as a key factor for Taiwan's greater involvement in the institutionalized regional economic integration. However, after the implementation of the ECFA in 2011, Taiwan's economy continued to suffer from weak external demand. The two economic agreements signed with New Zealand and Singapore were not expected to largely boost Taiwan's stagnant economy due to their small shares in Taiwan's external trade. Without clear progress in economic growth and significant expansion of Taiwan's FTA network, the Ma administration's active pursuit of economic engagement with China encountered deadlock after the Sunflower Student Movement in 2014. More details about Taiwan-China economic engagements are analyzed in Chap. 2.

Unlike President Ma, the Tsai administration does not consider greater cross-strait economic integration as the solution to rescue Taiwan's weak economy. As China's economy is also facing downward pressure, Taiwan has to diversify its economic dependence from China in order to minimize the potential economic risks. It is also to prevent Taiwan's strong economic dependence on China from being used as a political leverage. Tsai intends to reduce Taiwan's economic dependence on China through the "New Southward Policy". Unlike the "Southward Policy" in the 1990s, this "New Southward Policy" incorporates countries not only in Southeast Asia but also in South Asia. The policy focuses on enhancing bilateral economic relations as well as on seeking cooperation in other areas such as climate change, disease prevention, and disaster assistance. The DPP government also plans to increase civilian exchange via the means of Taiwanese citizens with spouses from Southeast Asia. China's booming economy may explain the ineffectiveness of Taiwan's "Southward Policy" during the 1990s. With rising labor costs and the slowing down of China's economy in recent years, Tsai's "New Southward Policy" may fit in with the current trend of relocating factories from China to other developing countries in Southeast Asia and India. Nonetheless, China still remains Taiwan's largest ODI destination and most important trading partner. This close economic tie cannot be changed in a short period of time. In this regard, the continued effort in finalizing free trade in goods and services agreements with China remains critical.

Given its huge consumption market, an economic engagement with the US is another essential factor for Taiwan's future economic prosperity. A Taiwan-US FTA could also encourage other countries to initiate trade negotiations with Taiwan. Taiwan-US economic talks were initiated as early as in 1994 through the Trade and Investment Framework Agreement (TIFA). TIFA had served as a platform for Taiwan to consult on a broad range of trade, investment, and economic issues prior to its entry to WTO. For the US, TIFA was a way to bring Taiwan in line with America's interests in exports and to access Taiwan's market. Between 1994 and 1998, major issues discussed included Taiwan's opening up of its agricultural, pharmaceutical, and telecommunications sectors within the WTO framework, Taiwan's Intellectual Property Rights (IPR) and the possibility of Taiwan joining the OECD. After 1998, the US suspended bilateral talks several times to express its dissatisfaction with the slow progress of Taiwan's IPR protection efforts, pharmaceutical pricing, and Taiwan's refusal to open up its rice and telecommunications markets. The bilateral talks resumed in 2004 after Taiwan's Legislative Yuan passed crucial amendments to the Copyright Law and Taiwan's tremendous progress in cracking down on commercial piracy. The scheduled TIFA talks in 2008 did not occur eventually due to Taiwan's ban on US beef containing ractopamine. To accede to US demand for deregulating the imports of American beef containing ractopamine, the Ma administration had urged Taiwan's Legislative Yuan to amend the law from zero tolerance of ractopamine to a defined limit on the amount permitted. Following Taiwan's lifting of the ban in July 2012, Taiwan's trade talks with the US resumed on 10 March 2013 (Chiang 2016). From 2013 to 2016, the bilateral talks through TIFA were conducted smoothly. A variety of issues have been under discussion. However, no significant agreement has been achieved so far.

The Taiwanese government considers the TIFA with America useful for its entry into the Trans-Pacific Partnership (TPP) and to further enhance Taiwan's substantive diplomacy. However, under President Trump's new economic agenda, the multilateral FTA has been downplayed. He withdrew the US from TPP in January 2017. The Trump administration has instead emphasized on the bilateral approach in economic relations with other countries. For a small economy like Taiwan, the trade talks through the bilateral approach are less advantageous than through a multilateral mechanism. Small countries do not have strong bargaining power in bilateral trade talks with big countries. On the other hand, small countries can cooperate together through a multinational mechanism when negotiating with big countries. The US withdrawal from the TPP also made Taiwan's entry into the TPP less possible. The other 11 countries are not strong supporters of Taiwan's entry into the TPP. It is still unclear whether China would join TPP. What is more certain is that the current TPP without the US is going to make the Regional Comprehensive Economic Partnership (RCEP) a more important multilateral economic agreement and China is the largest economy in RCEP.

Several studies have shown the economic disadvantages of being excluded from the multilateral FTAs. The negative effect tends to increase with the size of the multilateral FTAs. The negative impact also tends to be larger if China is a member of a multilateral FTA and Taiwan is not (Scollay and Gilbert 2001). The basic assumption is that the economic benefits generated by bilateral or multilateral FTAs signify an economic loss for the outsiders. For example, Chow's simulations result from the Global Trade Analysis Project (GTAP) model showed that Taiwan's GDP, exports, and economic welfare would decrease by 1.74 percent, 1.4 percent, and 0.73 percent respectively if six ASEAN countries (Indonesia,

Malaysia, the Philippines, Singapore, Thailand, and Vietnam), China, Hong Kong, South Korea, and Japan form a free trade area. The same study also showed Taiwan's GDP would increase by 2.09 percent and its exports would increase by 5.02 percent if Taiwan was included in this trading block (Chow and Ciuriak 2012). Nonetheless, as Taiwan is one of the WTO members, the generally low tariffs for the most favored nation (MFN) status under the WTO could minimize the impact of other multilateral FTAs on Taiwan. ICT products are Taiwan's most important export items. The Information Technology Agreement (ITA) under the WTO framework has already allowed Taiwan to export most of its ICT-related products to the signatory countries with zero tariffs. It is also argued that the utilization of other forms of FTAs may be low due to the costly requirements to demonstrate goods quality for the preferential treatment (Chow and Ciuriak 2012).

Taiwan has also attempted to initiate FTAs with other important trade partners such as Japan and Southeast Asian countries since the early 2000s. However, little progress has been made so far. To counterbalance the political constraint, Taiwan sought to initiate bilateral trade talks with different countries through the "bottom-up" approach. This means that Taiwan began trade negotiation with less sensitive issues and in the form of "economic agreement", instead of FTA. For example, Taiwan signed the "Agreement on the Liberalization, Promotion and Protection of Investment" and "Agreement on Mutual Cooperation on Electronic Commerce" with Japan in 2011 and 2013 respectively. The EU is also an important trade partner that Taiwan seeks to establish institutionalized economic relations with. In 2015, the EU commission stated that "the EU will explore launching negotiations on investment with Taiwan". "A Bilateral Investment Agreement (BIA) with Taiwan would go beyond investment protection, adopting a comprehensive approach with respect to market access as well as to rules that improve the overall regulatory framework" (European Union External Action 2016). Economic agreements with Israel, Indonesia, the Philippines, Malaysia, and India are under feasibility study.

South Korea's FTA Strategy: FTA as an Engine for Economic Growth

South Korea tended to support multilateral agreements, instead of bilateral FTAs before the 1990s. The government considered the former to be beneficial for Korea's exports whereas the latter could result in exclusive trading blocs that harm Korea's exports. It was not until the late 1990s that the Korean government changed its perception and actively sought to sign bilateral FTAs with other countries (Ahn 2010; Ge and Chen 2016; Liou 2013). The change in external trade policy began since the Kim administration in 1998. The Roh Moo-hyun administration (2003–2008) shifted Kim's cautious FTA policy into a more pro-active one. The Korean government hoped that extensive FTAs could strengthen Korea's export competitiveness and attract more foreign investment to the country. It also expected that FTAs would increase economic efficiency. Beyond the economic reasons, President Roh also regarded FTAs as a strategic tool to retain Korean interests in the evolving geopolitical and geoeconomic environment (Yoshimatsu 2012). Overall, Korea's FTA expansion policy is part of the national development strategy. Unlike Taiwan's diplomatic restraint, South Korea can use FTAs as leverage to strengthen its diplomatic relations.

In 2003, the Roh administration adopted the "FTA Promotion Roadmap" and classified potential countries with which to sign FTA in the short, medium, and long term. The small countries such as Chile and Singapore were classified as immediate FTA partners. The medium-sized countries such as Japan, Canada, and Mexico were categorized as the medium-term FTA partners. The long-term FTA partners included the US, EU, and India (Yoshimatsu 2012). Under the Roh administration, Korea signed FTAs with Chile, Singapore, Free Trade Agreement between the Member States of the European Free Trade Association (EFTA) and ASEAN. The above FTAs took effect between 2004 and 2009 (Table 5.2). With much support from big businesses, the Lee Myung-bak administration (2008–2013) continued to expand the number of FTAs. "Global Korea" and "pragmatism" were the two key concepts in Lee's foreign trade policy. Lee successfully helped Korea progress from "immediate FTA partners" to "medium- and long-term FTA partners" such as India, the US, and the EU.

South Korea's economic partnership agreement with India took effect since 1 January 2010. In 2011, it further implemented FTAs with the EU and Peru respectively. Nonetheless, the trade negotiation process with the US (KORUS FTA) was far more difficult than expected. Although the KORUS FTA was officially signed in 2007, it took almost five years for the agreement to be put into force eventually. The two most contentious issues involved the agriculture and automobile industries. Security concerns eventually pushed the two countries to renegotiate on

Table 5.2 South Korea's FTAs

	Type of agreement	*Implementation data*	*As % of Korea's exports in 2016*	*As % of Korea's imports in 2016*
Chile	FTA	1 April 2004	0.3	0.9
Singapore	FTA	2 March 2006	2.5	1.7
Free Trade Agreement between the Member States of the European Free Trade Association (EFTA)	FTA	1 September 2006	0.8	1.0
ASEAN	FTA	1 September 2009	15.0	10.9
India	Economic partnership	1 January 2010	2.3	1.0
EU	FTA	1 July 2011	9.5	12.8
Peru	FTA	1 August 2011	0.2	0.3
US	FTA	15 March 2012	13.4	10.6
China	FTA	20 December 2015	25.1	21.4
Total			69.1	60.6

Source: Ministry of Foreign Affairs (ROK) (n.d.)
Note: 1. EFTA includes Iceland, Norway, Liechtenstein, and Switzerland

the trade deal. After the Cheonan incident (South Korea navy sinking) in March 2010 and North Korea's sudden artillery attacks on South Korea in November of the same year, the urgent need to cement a security alliance to tackle the growing threat from the North propelled the two countries to relaunch stalled trade negotiations. On 3 December 2010, US President Obama and South Korean President Lee announced consensus on the outstanding issues in the FTA. The final agreement saw Korea granting further concessions on automobile and agricultural issues (Chiang 2017).

President Park Geun-hye's FTA policy was not very much different compared with the previous administrations. Her main achievement was the implementation of FTA with China in 2015. Since Korea has already implemented FTAs with the US and the EU, its FTA with China is considered to put Korea in a central position, connecting the American, European, and East Asian economies and benefiting its own economy in the long term. As mentioned in Chap. 2, 92 percent of South Korea's export items and 93 percent of China's will enjoy zero tariffs in bilateral trade in 20 years, except automobiles, petrochemical products, and rice which remain excluded from tariff reduction. The slow pace of full implementation and the limited width of tariff cuts suggest that bilateral trade in goods is not key to this bilateral FTA. Indeed, the two countries have sought to expand economic cooperation beyond traditional processing trade through this FTA. Korea expects to gain greater access to the Chinese market for Korean consumer goods and service business with China's push for a consumption-based economy. Although the tariff reduction in merchandise trade is limited, the two sides have committed to cooperate in other areas to enhance bilateral trade and industrial integration. In particular, the inclusion of products manufactured in the Kaesong Industrial Complex (located in North Korea) in the FTA is expected to contribute to the growth and stability of the Korean peninsula. In the long term, the industrial cooperation and further liberalization in investment and services are expected to enhance the connections between the two economies further. Geopolitically, the FTA could also play a role in achieving the two countries' regional development goals by linking Korea's Eurasia initiatives with China's "One Belt, One Road" plan (Chiang 2017).

President Moon Jae-in took office in 2017 amid the tough economic condition at home and volatile relations in the region. The geopolitical situation in the Korean Peninsula has become increasingly unstable following North Korea's continuous missile programs. At the same time, Japan and China have been expanding their maritime and defense activities in the region. The US role in the Asia-Pacific is also changing. Washington has withdrawn from the TPP and expects its allies to pay more for their military defense. To address the geopolitical and economic concerns, the US-South Korea Summit took place at the end of June 2017. Although the two countries' leaders have stressed the importance of bilateral alliance, Trump further emphasized sharing the cost of defense. Regardless of Trump's public criticism of South Korea's trade surplus with the US, Moon said that the agreement benefits both countries (Reuters 30 June 2017). Still, the Moon administration was not able to decline the US request for a renegotiation of the KORUS FTA. The renegotiation is expected to begin in the second half of 2018 after the completion of the renegotiation of the North American Free Trade Agreement (NAFTA) (The Hankyoreh 2 May 2017a). The Korean Economic Research Institute predicted a loss of about US$17 billion if the KORUS FTA is revised (Yonhap News Agency 25 May 2017).

Korea's relations with China have been worsening after Korea's decision to deploy the US-made Terminal High Altitude Area Defense (THAAD) in 2016. Korea considered the deployment of THAAD as necessary in the face of growing military threat from the North while China insisted that THAAD posed a security concern to its territory. China responded by implementing several economic sanctions against Korean businesses. China banned Korean entertainment services and a variety of products in its market. In 2017, Lotte Group announced plans to abandon its chain of hypermarkets and supermarkets in China after months of economic pressure from Beijing. Korea's cultural and retailing sectors and cars makers have reported significant declining business sales in China. The number of Chinese tourists to Korea also nosedived by 50 percent in 2017 (January–September). Moon sought to mend fences with China through the launch of a bilateral strategic economic dialogue and an increase in military exchanges. A South Korean government delegation to China's Belt and Road Summit in May 2017 was seen as efforts to restore diplomatic channels between South Korea and China in order to improve relations (The Hankyoreh 13 May 2017b). To ease China's anger, Korea's foreign minister announced in November 2017 that it will not deploy additional THAAD units nor would it participate in a US-led regional missile defense system or develop a military alliance with Japan and the US. Nonetheless, the different outlook toward the Korean Peninsula will continue to set South Korea politically apart from China. South Korea has been firm about THAAD's deployment whereas China would like it removed. In the meantime, China does not seem willing to exert extra pressure on the North Korean regime. China may consider North Korea as a buffer zone for maintaining China's geopolitical interests.

With Japan, Moon pledged to spearhead trade liberalization in the Asia-Pacific region by sealing the South Korea-China-Japan FTA. He also vowed to formulate a security regime among the three through the trilateral FTA. Overall, the Moon administration plans to return trade issues to the charge of the foreign ministry, from the Ministry of Trade, Industry and Energy (Yonhap News Agency 25 May 2017). A mixed strategy that combines both trade and geopolitical considerations is expected to be put into practice in the next five years.

Comparison of Taiwan and South Korea's Merchandise Trade Development

Taiwan's and South Korea's external trade has progressed smoothly over the last two decades. As shown in Fig. 5.1, Taiwan's merchandise trade surplus has increased gradually from US$21 billion in 2006 to US$50 billion in 2016. In comparison, South Korea's merchandise trade surplus has experienced a much higher growth. After the GFC, Korea's merchandise trade surplus grew from nearly US$15 billion in 2007 to US$40 billion in 2009 and US$89 billion in 2016. Korea's more extensive FTA might have bolstered quick development of trade surplus in goods. Unlike Taiwan, Korea has secured some important markets in the world through FTAs with the US, EU, ASEAN, and India.

China has been an important contributor to the development of Taiwan's merchandise trade surplus over the last two decades. Europe is the second largest source of Taiwan's trade surplus, followed by ASEAN and the US whereas Japan has remained Taiwan's largest source of trade deficit. As shown in Table 5.3, even though Taiwan has no FTA with China, the country has remained Taiwan's largest source of trade surplus. As mentioned in Chap. 2, the greater economic deregulations in bilateral trade and investment across the Strait after 2011 could have promoted the closer trade relations. Although the early harvest program under the ECFA covers only a limited number of products for free trade between

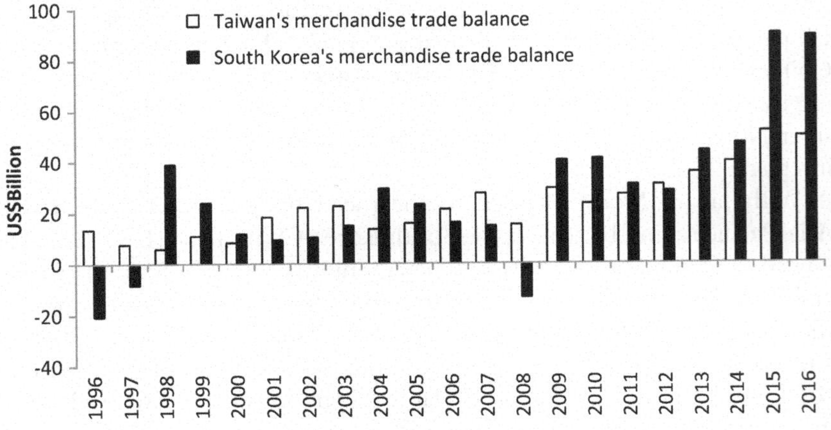

Fig. 5.1 Comparison of Taiwan and South Korea's merchandise trade balance 1996–2016. Source: Bureau of Foreign Trade, Taiwan; KOSIS

Taiwan and China, the ITA under the WTO has allowed Taiwan to export most of its ICT-related products to China and to other WTO member countries with low or zero tariffs. In recent years, however, Taiwan's exports to China have decelerated while its imports from China have become more prominent. As mentioned in Chap. 4, China's industrial catchup has resulted in Taiwan-made products becoming less competitive in the Chinese market. At the same time, the imports from China have been quickly increasing. As a consequence, Taiwan's trade surplus with China declined from US$80.4 billion in 2013 to US$67 billion in 2016.

China is also South Korea's largest source of trade surplus. Korea's trade surplus with China increased from US$37.8 billion in 2006 to US$88.6 billion in 2013. It started to decline to US$80.7 billion in 2014

Table 5.3 Taiwan and South Korea's merchandise trade balance by country/region 2006–2016

	Europe	*China and Hong Kong*	*Japan*	*ASEAN*	*US*
Taiwan's merchandise trade balance with major trading partners					
2006	19.5	63.4	−30.3	7.9	8.6
2007	25.7	71.3	−30.5	12.7	4.5
2008	13.6	67.6	−29.2	13.3	3.4
2009	28.1	59.0	−22.1	10.8	4.5
2010	21.7	78.4	−34.3	13.2	4.9
2011	24.9	80.3	−33.9	19.0	8.8
2012	29.1	77.1	−28.7	25.2	7.5
2013	33.4	80.4	−24.3	26.2	4.2
2014	38.2	77.5	−21.8	25.4	5.1
2015	48.1	65.8	−19.3	22.6	5.3
2016	49.8	67.0	−21.1	24.1	4.9
South Korea's merchandise trade balance with major trading partners					
2006	19.2	37.8	−25.4	−1.6	9.5
2007	19.4	35.5	−29.9	1.2	8.5
2008	18.7	32.0	−32.7	3.3	7.9
2009	14.4	50.6	−27.7	2.4	8.6
2010	14.9	68.6	−36.1	3.3	9.4
2011	8.9	76.4	−28.6	11.5	11.6
2012	−0.7	84.1	−25.6	19.0	15.2
2013	−7.2	88.6	−25.4	19.9	20.6
2014	−10.2	80.7	−21.6	21.1	25.0
2015	−8.6	75.8	−20.3	21.5	25.9
2016	−5.4	68.5	−23.1	23.8	23.4

Source: CEIC and Ministry of Finance (2017)
Unit: US$ billion

and was US$68.5 billion in 2016. Like Taiwan, the declining trade surplus with China is a result of greater imports from the country. China's growing manufacturing strength can be seen from Korea's greater import of manufacturing goods from China. Electrical machinery, machinery, and iron and steel accounted for over half of Korea's imports from China. The China-Korea FTA has been put into force since 2015. It remains to be seen how the FTA will affect the bilateral trade.

South Korea's trade relations with other economies have changed after the signing of FTAs. For instance, after South Korea implemented its FTA with ASEAN in 2009, its trade surplus with ASEAN clearly increased from US$3.3 billion in 2010 to US$23.8 billion in 2016. The South Korean investment shift from China to Southeast Asia might have contributed to the rise of Korean exports to ASEAN. The investment-driven trade has accounted for a large portion of South Korea-ASEAN total trade. South Korea supplied intermediate goods to ASEAN chiefly for its own manufacturing bases in these countries. In 2015, 40 percent of Korea's exports to and 32 percent of its imports from ASEAN were machinery and electrical machinery. As many ASEAN countries are rich in natural resources, they are also South Korea's chief import sources for mineral fuels. South Korea's trade balance with the EU has turned from surplus to deficit since the bilateral FTA took effect in 2011. South Korea's imports of food and heavy industrial goods, such as aircraft and vehicles from the EU, have registered significant growth after the implementation of the bilateral FTA. South Korea's growing trade balance with the US shows that the KORUS FTA seems to have reinforced South Korea's comparative advantage in manufacturing. Korea's merchandise trade surplus with the US doubled from US$11.6 billion in 2011 to US$25.8 billion in 2015. Beyond the tariff cuts and greater investment liberalization under the KORUS FTA, the moderate growth of the US economy after the GFC is another factor for the stronger trade relations between the two countries. However, the sluggish economy in South Korea in recent years may have restrained the Korean consumption of US goods. The limited wage increase has also restrained Korean consumers' purchasing capacity.

Comparison of Taiwan's and South Korea's Service Trade Development

Unlike its growing merchandise trade surplus, South Korea's service trade deficit has worsened much more than Taiwan's over the last decade. As shown in Fig. 5.2, Taiwan's service trade deficit ranged between US$9

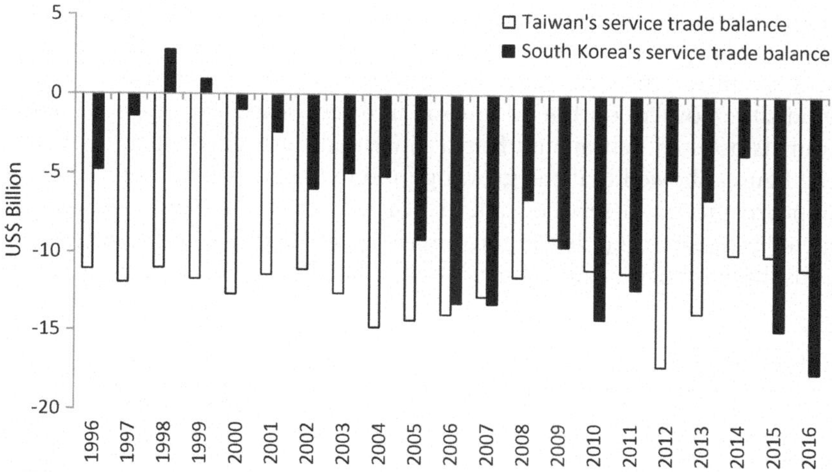

Fig. 5.2 Comparison of Taiwan and South Korea's service trade balance. Source: Taiwan's Central Bank (2017), KOSIS (2017)

billion and US$15 billion from 1996 to 2016. In comparison, South Korea's service trade deficit has clearly grown from US$1 billion in 2000 to US$17 billion in 2016. The FTAs were supposed to enhance the two countries' comparative advantages in manufacturing while opening up the less competitive services sector to foreign competition. As such, South Korea's greater involvement in the global economy through FTAs has improved its merchandise trade development. Meanwhile, the FTAs also facilitated other countries to enter into Korea's services market. However, services in South Korea are not strong enough to compete in the global market through the country's greater FTA network.

As mentioned in Chap. 4, Taiwan's and South Korea's services have failed to pick up the slack when the manufacturers faced weak external demand. Table 5.4 demonstrates Taiwan's and South Korea's service trade balance by items. Taiwan and South Korea ran trade deficits in almost all service items, implying that both economies still relied on other countries to provide services in support of their manufacturing production. Some features of Taiwan's and South Korea's service trade can be summarized as follows. First, Taiwan's and South Korea's deficit in manufacturing services implies that there is a strong demand for manufacturing services that domestic service firms do not provide. Manufacturing services include activities such as processing, assembly, labeling, and packing undertaken by enterprises that do not own the goods. Second, both countries' travel deficit shows their greater outbound tourist spending in overseas countries than the inbound tourist spending. Following China's gradual removal of outbound tourism in recent years, the surging Chinese tourists boosted Taiwan and Korea's inbound tourism receipts. However, the figures showed that the growing inbound tourists have not helped to improve the travel service trade deficit. Third, "other business", which includes research and development services, professional and management consulting services, and technical trade-related business services, has been

Table 5.4 Taiwan and South Korea's service trade balance by items

	2004	*2008*	*2012*	*2016*
Taiwan				
Manufacturing services	n/a	n/a	−7666	−1463
Transport	−2716	−1736	231	−1877
Travel	−4116	−3179	1140	−3191
Construction	−406	0	−119	20
Insurance services	−823	−661	−671	−426
Financial services	258	799	1336	1736
Charges for the use of intellectual property	−1387	−2824	−3581	−2166
Telecommunications, computer, and information services	−289	−208	−77	1041
Other business services	−4370	−2908	−6559	−4404
Personal, cultural, and recreational services	−189	−85	−125	92
Government services	−628	−553	−492	−330
South Korea				
Manufacturing services	−296	−3140	−6653	−5464
Transport	4548	7574	10,177	−628
Travel	−6281	−9306	−7216	−9432
Construction	2169	11,079	16,345	8688
Insurance services	−323	−277	−304	−234
Financial services	359	411	−436	56
Telecommunications, computer, and information services	−125	−440	1	843
Charges for the use of intellectual property	−2681	−3389	−4714	−2669
Maintenance and repair services	15	4	168	−4
Other business services	−3318	−9157	−12,770	−8867
Personal, cultural, and recreational services	−52	−173	−95	464
Government services	823	270	283	−361

Source: Central Bank of Taiwan (2017), KOSIS (2017)
Unit: US$ million

the largest source of Taiwan and Korea's service trade deficit. The large deficit in "other business" and "charges for IPR" suggests the two countries are still highly dependent on foreign technology and value-added services from advanced countries. Fourth, while most of Korea's service items were in deficit, its construction services had been registering a surplus since many decades ago. South Korea's construction firms had entered the global market since the 1970s, mainly in the Middle East (Kim 1988). The trade surplus in construction quickly developed since the 2000s. Finally, Taiwan's trade surplus in financial services has visible growth from US$258 million in 2004 to US$1736 million in 2016. The deregulation of financial services investment in China could be the reason. According to the early harvest program of the ECFA signed in June 2010, China agreed to open up the banking, insurance, securities, and futures sectors for Taiwanese investment with conditions, whereas Taiwan agreed to open up only the banking sector to China. As a result of the opening up measures in financial services, Taiwan's investments in China's financial sector began to grow steadily.

Conclusion

Given their different political and economic conditions, Taiwan's and Korea's respective approaches to pursue the expansion of an FTA network have been different. In Taiwan, the Ma administration sought to initiate FTA talks with other countries by forging institutionalized economic relations with China first. After the implementation of the early harvest program under the ECFA in 2011, the limited extension of Taiwan's FTA network and slow economic growth discredited President Ma's approach. In addition, the greater economic engagement with China was considered as a threat to the island's national security. Given its small economic size, Taiwan's economic reliance on China implies that any political confrontation with China would result in a greater impact on Taiwan's economy rather than vice versa. The deadlock in the CSSTA in Taiwan reflected the Taiwanese people's unease that deeper integration with China could not be offset by the potential economic gains. Tsai's election as Taiwan's president in 2016 could be interpreted as the people's wish to keep a distance from China. Unlike President Ma, Tsai vowed to revitalize the economy through diversifying Taiwan's economic relations from China to other countries. The "New Southward Policy" was launched in order to enhance Taiwan's overall relations with countries in Southeast Asia and India after

Tsai took office in 2016. The Tsai administration also seeks membership in the Regional Comprehensive Economic Partnership and Trans-Pacific Partnership. So far, Taiwan's extension of its FTA network is still progressing very slowly. China's continued political pressure on the Tsai administration would make its "active diplomacy" and "economic diversification" even more difficult to be realized. There can be little doubt that cross-Strait relations are of key importance to Taiwan's economic relations with foreign partners. Nevertheless, all of this would matter less when trade liberalization takes place largely in the context of the WTO of which Taiwan is also a member.

Unlike Taiwan, South Korea today is at the forefront of the Asia-Pacific FTA trend. Korea's active FTA projects were deemed integral to the Kim government's post-crisis restructuring agenda. The successors after Kim generally followed the economic opening up through actively pursuing FTAs talks with other trading partners. South Korea's launch of an extensive FTA network to gain greater access to foreign markets has successfully promoted the country's external trade development over the last two decades. The network is especially important for South Korea to explore new avenues to sustain its export-led growth when China's economy is on the downward trend in recent years. The official statistics indicate that Korea's merchandise trade surplus has been progressing after the GFC. However, its trade deficit in services has enlarged since the latter half of the 2000s. This shows that Korea's large manufacturing giants benefited from the greater economic opening up. On the other hand, its less competitive services sector has suffered from the growing foreign competition. From a positive point of view, although it is inevitable that the less qualified workers and less competitive services at home would suffer from the economic opening up, the FTAs will make it more attractive for foreign investors who will make up for the limited job supply from chaebols. Likewise, Korean SMEs could seek to improve on their competitiveness and benefit from the "technology transfer" from foreign investors in the West.

References

Ahn, D. (2010). FTA policy and Strategy of Korea. *Taiwanese Journal of WTO Studies, XV*, 39–66.

Bureau of Foreign Trade (Taiwan). (2017). Retrieved June 13, 2017, from http://fta.trade.gov.tw/index.asp

CEIC Global Database. (2017). Retrieved September 28, 2017, from https://www.ceicdata.com/zh-hans

Central Bank of Republic of China (Taiwan). (2017). Retrieved March 2, 2018, from https://www.cbc.gov.tw/np.asp?ctNode=507&mp=2

Cheung, F. K., Lee, M. L., & Wu, Y.-C. (1997). Endogenous export prices and the Taiwan-US trade imbalance. *Applied Economics, 29*(1), 23–31.

Chiang, M.-H. (2016). *China-Taiwan Rapprochement: The politicl economy of cross-strait relations*. London: Routledge.

Chiang, M.-H. (2017). *Contemporary South Korea economy: Challenges and prospects*. Singapore: World Scientific.

Chow, P. C. Y., & Ciuriak, D. (2012). The FTA music is playing in Asia: After ECFA, will Taiwan join the dance? *The International Trade Journal, 26*(1), 61–75.

Dent, C. M. (2002). *The foreign economic policies of Singapore, South Korea and Taiwan*. Cheltenham and Northampton: Edward Elgar.

Dent, C. M. (2006). *New free trade agreements in the Asia-Pacific*. Hampshire and New York: Palgrave Macmillan.

European Union External Action. (2016, May 17). Taiwan and the EU. Retrieved October 2, 2017, from https://eeas.europa.eu/headquarters/headquarters-homepage_en/2000/Taiwan%20and%20the%20EU

Ge, Y., & Chen, G.-Y. (2016). South Korea's FTA strategy on the Korea-US Free Trade Agreement (han guo yu mei guo qian ding zi you mao yi xie ding zhan lue zhi yan jiu). *Issues and Studies, 55*(3), 1–40.

Kim, S. (1988). The Korean construction industry as an exporter of services. *The World Bank Economic Review, 2*(2), 225–238.

Korean Statistical Information Service (KOSIS). (2017). Statistics Korea. Retrieved March 2, 2018, from http://kosis.kr/eng/

Liou, T.-H. (2013). South Korea's FTA strategy and its implications for economic integration in Northeast Asia. *Journal of International Politics and Economics, 1*, 1–20.

Ministry of Finance (Taiwan). (2017). Monthly statistics. Retrieved May 8, 2017, from https://www.mof.gov.tw/List/Index?nodeid=281&ban=Y

Ministry of Foreign Affairs (Republic of Korea). (n.d.). Retrieved June 13, 2017, from http://www.mofat.go.kr/ENG/policy/fta/status/effect/chile/index.jsp?menu=m_20_80_10&tabmenu=t_2

Reuters (2017, June 30). Trump calls for firm response to North Korea, target Seoul on trade. Retrieved July 16, 2017, from http://www.reuters.com/article/us-usa-southkorea-idUSKBN19L27E

Scollay, R., & Gilbert, J. P. (2001). *New regional trading arrangements in the Asia Pacific*. Washington: Institute for International Economics.

The Hankyoreh. (2017a, May 2). Trump's rumblings on KORUS FTA a chance to address poisonous clauses. Retrieved May 31, 2017, from http://english.hani.co.kr/arti/english_edition/e_business/793183.html

The Hankyoreh (2017b, May 13). China invites South Korean government delegation to Belt and Road summit. Retrieved May 31, 2017, from http://english.hani.co.kr/arti/english_edition/e_international/794583.html
Yonhap News Agency (2017, May 25). Foreign ministry to reclaim trade negotiation task amid looming FTA revision with US. Retrieved May 31, 2017, from http://english.yonhapnews.co.kr/national/2017/05/25/91/0301000000AEN20170525010700315F.html
Yoshimatsu, H. (2012). Political leaders' preferences and trade policy: Comparing FTA politics in Japan and South Korea. *Asian Politics & Policy.*, *4*(2), 193–212.

CHAPTER 6

New Challenges Ahead (I): Growing Income Inequality

Abstract This chapter identified the hollowing out of manufacturing production, greater importance of large firms in the economy, employees' wage stagnation, and rising housing prices as main reasons for the growing income inequality in Taiwan and South Korea. These factors are related. The hollowing out of manufacturing production is a result of massive investment in developing countries. Large firms benefited from their overseas investment while most of the domestic labors could only shift to low value-added service jobs with less remuneration. The wealthy entrepreneurs returned back to home countries and invested in real estate that led to higher housing prices. In the future, the majority of people with minor income would erode private consumption. The growing income inequality could also become a more serious concern in the societies if the economy continues to grow slowly.

Keywords Income inequality • Gini coefficient • Hollowing of manufacturing production • Wage stagnation • Household debt

The growing income disparity has recently become a societal concern in both Taiwan and South Korea. Although the Gini index in both countries is not dire when compared with other countries, many people in Taiwan and South Korea increasingly feel the strains of an unfair distribution of income. A local newspaper survey in Taiwan in 2014 indicated

M.-H. Chiang, *Post-Industrial Development in East Asia*,
https://doi.org/10.1007/978-981-13-0274-9_6

that 85 percent of people considered the gap between the rich and the poor to be enlarging. The 2013 Social Survey done by the Korean government showed that among the population aged above 19 years, nearly half were dissatisfied with their income. Only 14 percent were satisfied with their consumption ability. Economically, insufficient disposable income for the majority of the population could dampen domestic consumption and economic growth prospects. Politically, the unequal income distribution could lead to social instability. As such, making wealth distribution more equitable is not only an economic issue but also an important political task.

However, the survey result is debatable. People would feel no better off if they had recognized that their relative position had not improved. The declining attachment to communities and jobs and the increasing influence of the media also encourage comparison with the rich and famous rather than those around us. Since the majority of people are falling behind those at the top, such comparison only yields increasing dissatisfaction (Glyn 2006). The purpose of this chapter is to explore the severity of income inequality in Taiwan and South Korea and the reasons for the growing income inequality. The chapter is organized as follows. The first section compares the income inequality in both countries in quantitative terms. Next, several factors that contributed to the income inequality are analyzed: the hollowing out of the manufacturing sector, wage differences between large companies and SMEs, wage stagnation for employees, and rising housing prices. These factors are discussed respectively in the following sections. Finally, major findings and key points are summarized in the conclusion.

Measuring Income Inequality

The Gini coefficient is a commonly used measure for income inequality. In general, the higher the number, the worse the income inequality is. Compared with the ratios a decade ago, Taiwan's Gini coefficient increased from 0.291 in 1985 to 0.317 in 1995, 0.340 in 2005, and 0.338 in 2015. South Korea's Gini coefficient for urban households increased relatively insignificantly from 0.259 in 1995 to 0.307 in 2013 and slowed down to 0.295 in 2015. Compared with some European countries, Taiwan's Gini coefficient today is relatively high. European countries such as France, Germany, and Norway have relatively low Gini coefficients (Table 6.1). Nonetheless, the figures are relatively low compared with most of the

Table 6.1 International comparison of Gini coefficients in 2014

Country	*Gini coefficient*
Asia-Pacific	
Australia	0.337
China	0.421**
Japan	0.330
South Korea	**0.295***
Taiwan	**0.338***
Singapore	0.463*
Hong Kong	0.521*
North and South America	
Canada	0.322
Chile	0.465
US	0.394
Mexico	0.459
Europe	
UK	0.358
Italy	0.325
France	0.294
Germany	0.292
Norway	0.252

Source: DGBAS and OECD income distribution database
Note: "*" refers to figures in 2015, "**" refers to figure in 2010

countries in the Asia-Pacific region and South America. China, Singapore, and Hong Kong in Asia and Chile and Mexico in South America have particularly higher Gini coefficients.

Due to its oversimplification and exclusion of personal wealth from other sources, it is often argued that the Gini coefficients may not provide an accurate picture of a country's income inequality problem (World Bank 2016). Moreover, the income inequality figures do not seem to match reality, suggesting a larger problem than what the figures can reflect. For example, in Taiwan, the official household survey was often criticized for its inaccuracy because the high-income earners are not compelled to reveal their real financial status.

The data from the World Wealth and Income Database provides an alternative way to investigate the income inequality problem in each country. As shown in Table 6.2, the richest 1 percent of Taiwan's total population earned 11.3 percent of total fiscal income in 2012 whereas in South Korea, the ratio is 12.2 percent. Both countries' ratios have clearly

Table 6.2 Top 1% and top 10% of high-income population's share in the fiscal income in Taiwan and South Korea 1995–2013

	Top 1% share in fiscal income		*Top 10% share in fiscal income*	
	Taiwan	*South Korea*	*Taiwan*	*South Korea*
1995	7.3	6.9	28.8	29.2
1996	7.3	7.3	29.2	32.6
1997	7.5	7.5	29.3	33.4
1998	8.0	6.6	30.7	31.4
1999	7.9	7.5	29.7	33.4
2000	8.9	8.2	31.3	35.4
2001	9.1	8.6	32.5	36.3
2002	8.6	9.2	30.4	38.0
2003	9.2	9.2	31.0	38.7
2004	9.1	9.6	31.7	39.5
2005	9.9	10.0	33.4	37.8
2006	9.9	10.8	33.5	41.9
2007	10.8	11.3	35.3	42.4
2008	11.4	11.4	36.9	42.9
2009	9.7	11.3	33.7	42.6
2010	11.2	11.8	36.4	43.3
2011	11.7	12.2	37.6	44.2
2012	11.3	12.2	38.2	44.9
2013	n/a	n/a	36.4	n/a

Source: World Wealth and Income Database

increased from a respective 7.3 percent and 6.9 percent in 1995. The top 10 percent of the population in Taiwan earned 36.4 percent of total fiscal income in 2013, from 28.8 percent in 1995. In South Korea, the figure is more significant. A total of 44.9 percent of fiscal income was earned by the top 10 percent of the population in 2012, from 29.2 percent in 1995. In sum, the figures income for the top 1 percent and top 10 percent in both countries have shown significant growth compared to two decades ago.

Following the worsening issue of income distribution is the growing poverty problem. The relative poverty rate is defined as the share of the population living with less than half of the median income. In South Korea, the poverty rate shows a surging trend from 8.7 percent in 1997 to 14.5 percent in 2013. The official figures also indicated that, from 2011 to 2013, more than 3 million people fell into relative poverty with US$18,000 of annual income or less. The poverty problem is particularly serious among the elderly. In 2013, the relative poverty rate for those aged 65 and above stood at 48 percent respectively, much higher than the national average (14.5 percent) (Chiang 2017). In Taiwan, there are no official figures showing the poverty rate. We can take a look at the poverty problem through the official household survey. According to the survey, a household with monthly income below NT$11,448 (about US$382) is categorized as low income. In 2015, the official statistics from the Ministry of Health and Welfare showed that there were 146,379 low-income households. A total of 342,490 people came from low-income families, which is about 1.5 percent of Taiwan's total population.

Growing Income Inequality After the Hollowing Out of Manufacturing Production

No matter how the figures for income inequality are calculated and estimated, one thing for sure is the clear trend toward greater income inequality. An important question is: what are the driving factors for the greater income inequality in Taiwan and South Korea over the last two decades? The massive ODI to the developing countries could be an important reason. Although the relocation of manufacturing production to other developing countries allowed Taiwan and Korea to upgrade domestic industries at home, the job opportunities in services were not able to meet the demand from all the laid-off manufacturing sector workers. As Taiwan and South Korea struggled to maintain their competitiveness in producing middle- to high-technology goods in the regional supply chain network, the unskilled labor at home lost their jobs in the labor-intensive manufacturing sector. The higher technological level and productivity at home also means that fewer domestic workers are needed. The unemployment rate began to rise as a result.

Over the last two decades, the unemployment rates in Taiwan and South Korea have remained relatively low (around 3–4 percent) compared with advanced countries except during the crisis period. In absolute terms, however, the numbers are more shocking. Among the total labor force, the unemployed population in Taiwan increased from 165,000 in 1995 to 440,000 in 2015 (National Development Council 2016). In South Korea, the number of unemployed rose from 419,000 to 976,000 during the same period (Data source: CEIC and KOSIS). When several manufacturing industries were moved overseas, many domestic workers shifted to low-value-added sectors with lower wages. A comparison of employment across different sectors can prove this argument. The number of employees and the average monthly wages in 2005 and 2015 in Taiwan's different sectors are compared in Table 6.3. There were 2,479,000 employees in the manufacturing sector in 2005. This figure increased to 2,717,000 in 2015, a growth of 238,000 people. In comparison, the industries that offered average monthly wages higher than manufacturing saw an increase of employment by 240,000 people. In particular, medical and human health had the highest growth in employment (102,000), followed by professional, scientific, and technical services (76,000). However, the employment in industries with average monthly wages lower than manufacturing increased by 710,000 people. The wholesale and retail trade and accommodation and food services had the highest growth of employment (186,000 and 177,000 people respectively) during 2005 and

Table 6.3 Taiwan's average monthly wages and employment by sector in 2005 and 2015

	No. of employees (1000 people)			*Average monthly wages (NT$)*
	2005	*2015*	*Increase (+) or decrease (−)*	
1. Electricity, gas supply	27	30	+3	96,444
2. Financial and insurance	369	375	+6	84,696
3. Information and communication	165	196	+31	66,453
4. Medical and human health	233	335	+102	64,103
5. Professional, scientific, and technical services	177	253	+76	58,252
6. Mining and quarrying	6	4	−2	53,886
7. Transportation and storage	260	284	+24	51,219
Subtotal 1–7	**1237**	**1477**	**+240**	**n/a**
8. Manufacturing	**2479**	**2717**	**+238**	**46,781**
9. Wholesale and retail trade	1455	1641	+186	45,488
10. Water supply and pollution control	21	28	+7	44,183
11. Construction	400	461	+61	43,346
12. Real estate	71	117	+46	42,351
13. Arts, entertainment, and leisure services	45	56	+11	36,185
14. Business support services	192	342	+150	35,671
15. Other services	88	160	+72	34,526
16. Accommodation and food services	213	390	+177	32,596
Subtotal 9–16	**2485**	**3195**	**+710**	**n/a**

Source: National Statistics, Taiwan

2015 among the lower wages group. Overall, this demonstrated a greater number of employment shifted to services with lower wages during the 2005–2015 period.

A similar trend can be found in South Korea. As shown in Table 6.4, only 834,000 more workers found more lucrative jobs (items 1–6) while 2,268,000 had to contend with lower paying jobs (items 8–17) compared to their counterparts in the manufacturing industries. Between 2005 and 2015, the services sector took in six times more workers (2,268,000) at a lower pay than what the manufacturing sector (356,000) had hired and

Table 6.4 South Korea's average monthly wages and employment by sector in 2005 and 2015

	No. of employees (1000 people)			*Average monthly wages in 2015 (KRW)*
	2005	*2015*	*Increase (+) or decrease (−)*	
1. Electricity, gas, steam, and water supply	71	93	+22	5,913,989
2. Financial and insurance	745	789	+44	5,580,308
3. Professional, scientific, and technical activities	625	1048	+423	4,628,852
4. Information and communication	638	772	+134	4,154,984
5. Education	1604	1818	+214	3,857,553
6. Mining and quarrying	17	14	−3	3,793,870
Subtotal 1–6	**3700**	**4534**	**+834**	**n/a**
7. Manufacturing	**4130**	**4486**	**+356**	**3,671,757**
8. Wholesale and retail trade	3746	3783	+37	3,397,174
9. Construction	1813	1823	+10	3,240,406
10. Sewage & water treatment	56	88	+32	3,028,148
11. Transportation	1165	1409	+244	3,006,245
12. Arts, sports, and recreation services	383	424	+41	2,989,518
13. Human health and social work	639	1770	+1131	2,847,015
14. Membership organization, repair, and other personal services	1171	1277	+106	2,589,661
15. Real estate, renting, and leasing	496	535	+39	2,505,484
16. Accommodation and food services	2058	2179	+121	2,235,380
17. Business facilities management and business support services	742	1249	+507	2,096,821
Subtotal 8–17	**12,269**	**14,537**	**2268**	**n/a**

Source: KOSIS

almost triple that of industries with wages higher than that of the manufacturing industries. Human health and social work had the highest growth in terms of the increased number of workers (1,131,000), followed by workers in business facilities and business support services (507,000) and transportation (244,000). Among the industries with wages higher than in manufacturing, the professional, scientific, and technical industries received the highest increase in employment (423,000). In comparison, employment in high-value-added services such as financial and insurance registered relatively lower increase (44,000).

Wage Differences by Company's Size and by Type of Contract

The wage differences can also be found by different company sizes. As mentioned in Chap. 3, the SMEs are the main contributor to domestic employment in both Taiwan and South Korea. Nonetheless, their limited profit margin constrains them from offering higher remuneration for their domestic workers. As such, wage dispersion between large companies and SMEs with a bigger workforce has enlarged the income inequality. The wage differences between large and small companies are particularly clear in South Korea. The average monthly wage for Korean workers of large companies (more than 300 employees) was 4,645,000 won (US$4312) in 2014, up from 3,787,000 won (US$3516) in 2008. In comparison, the average monthly wage of workers in small companies (5–9 employees) increased from 1,834,000 won (US$1527) in 2008 to 2,238,000 won (US$1863) in 2014. Although monthly wages for workers in SMEs improved annually, the wage gap with large companies remains unchanged (Data source: CEIC). The wages in top chaebols were even higher. In 2012, for example, the average monthly wage for workers at Samsung was 4.46 million won (US$3753), twice the average monthly wage for workers with similar skills at SMEs in the electronics industry (2 million won or US$1683) (Han et al. 2013). The growing number of workers at SMEs made the income inequality more obvious. From 2000 to 2014, the number of employees at SMEs increased by 5,346,942 whereas the number with large firms declined by 152,794 (Data source: Ministry of SMEs and Startups).

Beyond company size, the labor market dualism is another factor that has enlarged wage dispersion in Korea. South Korea's employment is categorized into three major types: regular workers, non-regular workers, and self-employed people. Regular workers refer to those with a regular contract, better salary, and better social protection. Non-regular workers include temporary employees, family workers, and daily-rated workers. They are usually paid less than regular employees for the same job duties. After the AFC, the number of non-regular workers saw a clear rise while that of regular workers declined. The "labor flexibility" policy implemented by Kim Dae-jung in 1998 drove up the statistics for non-regular workers. The market-based labor rules were supposedly directed at particular forms of skilled labor. Nonetheless, companies increasingly took advantage of the legalization of temporary work agencies in 1998 and subcontracted work to work agencies to avoid the legal obligations. The rise of non-regular workers contributed to the slowdown of unemployment problems after the crisis. The unemployment rate declined from 6.3 percent in 1999 to 3.6 percent in 2003. During the same period, the share of non-regular workers was maintained at a high of between 40 percent and 42 percent of total employment whereas the share of regular workers was between 30 percent and 33 percent. The self-employed hovered between 27 percent and 28 percent. As non-regular workers were usually paid less than regular employees for the same job duties, the wage gap was enlarging. Even worse, the non-regular workers are more numerous in SMEs than in large firms. Non-regular workers' wages are less than 60 percent of regular workers' in SMEs (Korea Institute for a New Society 2016).

Various measures have been taken to tackle labor market dualism in recent years. In 2011, the government launched the "Comprehensive Non-regular Workers Initiatives" to address the dualism problem by strengthening the social safety net and promoting equal treatment for non-regular workers (Randall and Satoshi 2013). In 2013, the government announced a plan to convert around 26 percent of fixed-term workers in the public sector to regular status by 2015. Private firms were also encouraged to grant regular contract to non-regular employees partly through tax incentives (Randall and Satoshi 2013). With the policy initiatives, the number of non-regular workers with inferior wages and less protection from social insurance gradually decreased. Despite the improvement, the latest figure shows that there were still 7,919,000 non-regular workers in June 2017, which was about 30 percent of total employment. The regular workers and self-employed workers accounted for a respective 49 percent and 21 percent of total employment (Data source: KOSIS).

Compared to South Korea, the wage difference between SMEs and large firms in Taiwan is relatively less obvious. According to official statistics, the average monthly wage for workers at SMEs in manufacturing industries was NT$34,650 (US$1155) in 2015 whereas in large companies, it was NT$40,230 (US$1341). In the services sector, the wage difference is especially large in professional, scientific, and technical supporting services. The difference was NT$18,080 (US$603). In all the sectors, the difference of average monthly wage for workers at SMEs and large companies was NT$8612 (about US$287) (Data source: Small and Medium Enterprise Administration 2016). The smaller difference in wages in Taiwan could be reasoned by the lesser profits earned by large companies than Korean chaebols. Compared to South Korea, the gap between the number of employees at SMEs and large companies is also less obvious. The number of employees at SMEs increased by nearly 2 million from 1995 to 2015 whereas the employees at large companies increased by 590,000 during the same period (Small and Medium Enterprise Administration 1998, 2006, 2016).

Unlike Korea, the pool of temporary workers or "dispatched labor" in Taiwan has been developed only in recent years. In general, the dispatched workers bear the same duties as other regular employees in companies but they had working contracts with work agencies. Beyond the cost consideration, the "dispatched workers" provided firms with flexibility especially when the economic condition was uncertain. Even government agencies hired over 30,000 dispatched workers to carry out temporary job duties for particular events or projects. In 2016, the number of temporary workers was 1,824,000, increasing from 1,459,000 in 2008. The share of temporary workers in the total employment increased from 14 percent to 16 percent during the same period according to Ministry of Labor in Taiwan.

Employees' Wage Stagnation Versus Business Owners' Wealth Expansion

The growing income inequality could also be a result of stagnant income growth for the working-class employees and growing wealth for the business owners. The limited profit margin might have restrained many Taiwanese companies from raising wages for their workers. Another reason could be the low inflation rate. The government considered low inflation essential to maintain economic stability. For several decades, Taiwan's inflation rate has been kept at a relatively low level by subsidizing public companies in electricity and fuel. Low inflation rate means that wages can be kept low. Low wage was also attractive for foreign investors during Taiwan's post-war industrialization period. However, with the relocation of labor-intensive manufacturing production to China after the 1990s, the low wage has become a disadvantage. With wages inferior to other countries, many talents in high-value-added industries would rather work overseas to obtain better remuneration. The low wages also mean Taiwanese workers compete in an international labor market that also includes low-cost mainland Chinese workers.

As shown in Fig. 6.1, the annual growth rate of average monthly wages was less than 2 percent between 2000 and 2009 in Taiwan. Wages grew quickly in 2010 after the sharp decline in 2009. In comparison, South Korea's wages have seen a relatively higher growth than Taiwan's over the past 15 years. However, the annual growth rates of monthly wages in South Korea have also been declining in recent years. Between 2000 and 2007, the annual growth rate of monthly wages grew at 5–11 percent. The rates have been decelerating to between 2 percent and 5 percent during the 2012–2015 period.

The governments have responded to growing dissatisfaction of stagnant wages by raising minimum wages. The monthly minimum wage in

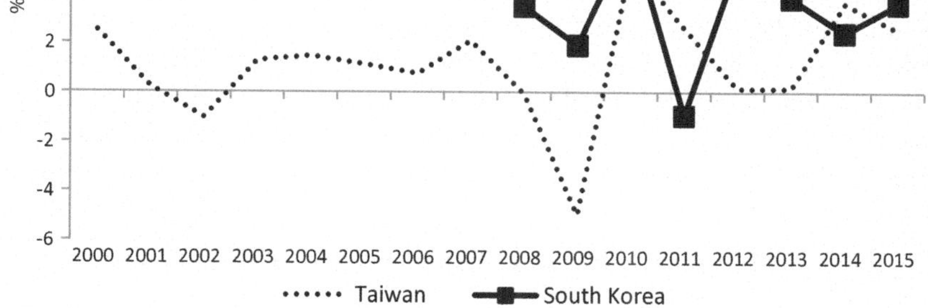

Fig. 6.1 Growth rate of monthly wages in Taiwan and South Korea 2000–2015. Source: DGBAS; Korea Statistical Yearbook, various years

Taiwan was increased from NT$20,008 (US$639) to NT$21,009 with effect from 2017. The government has set minimum wage at NT$140 (US$ 4.7) an hour and NT$22,000 (US$732.8) a month effective 1 January 2018. Minimum wage is applied to all domestic and foreign workers. Wages of public sector employees will also be increased by 3% from 2018, after a freeze of more than six years. Similarly, President Moon Jae-in in South Korea promised to increase minimum wages to 10,000 won (US$8.9) an hour by 2020 from the current 6470 won (US$5.8). In addition, he also called for reduction of working hours to 1800 a year, from an average of 2113 in 2015. Despite the salary adjustment, some have raised concerns about the pressure on enterprises especially during the economic slowdown. With the higher labor cost, small businesses fear their profits would be further eroded.

In contrast to the stagnation of workers' wages, business owners who have been able to extend their business operations in developing countries have become richer. In 2014, measured by sales revenue, 17 Korean conglomerates were listed in the Fortune 500 list, an increase from 14 in 2013. Korea ranks seventh among countries with the most global 500 companies (Yonhap News Agency July 8, 2014). The revenue has been captured by a few large chaebols. The country's top four conglomerates (Samsung, Hyundai Motors, SK, and LG) generated 90 percent of total net profits earned by the top 30 Korean conglomerates in 2013 (Nikkei Asian Review April 7, 2014). The increasingly profitable conglomerates gave rise to top-earning corporate executives. The 2014 list of the richest individuals in South Korea saw a record of 30 US dollar billionaires, up from 21 in 2011 and 5 in 2009. The aggregate wealth of Korean billionaires totaled US$82.6 billion in 2014, from US$65.6 billion in 2011 (Forbes 2011). In comparison, the business scale of Taiwanese companies is much smaller. Only eight Taiwanese companies are listed in the Fortune 500 list. According to Forbes, with US$8 billion of net wealth, the brothers who run Fubon Financial rank first among Taiwan's richest in 2016. For the others on the top ten richest ranking, six are engaged in manufacturing. The others are either in the real estate or in financial industries.

Rising Housing Prices Increasing Income Inequality

Housing prices have become increasingly unaffordable for residents in both countries in recent years. As the rise in housing prices has increased the wealth of homeowners, it has led to greater income inequality between the rich and the poor. A large number of rich people in Taiwan have accumulated their wealth by land sales. According to local media reports, among the 0.01 percent of the highest income group in Taiwan, 84 percent of their income came from capital gains and just 14 percent of their income from their regular salary (The Reporter August 6, 2016). Real estate also occupied an important share in the wealth of rich Koreans. In 2013, the average rich Korean's total assets consisted of 54.1 percent in real estate holdings, 39.6 percent in financial assets, and 6.3 percent in other assets (Noh et al. 2014).

According to Global Property Guide, after the fall of housing price in late 2008, Taiwan's volatile housing market experienced a quick recovery during 2009–2015. There are several reasons for the quick rise of housing prices. First, the low interest rate after the GFC contributed to the quick growth of housing prices. Second, the government's cut on inheritance tax rates from 50 percent to 10 percent in 2009 was another reason (Delmendo 2016). Third, there was a growing return of overseas Taiwanese financial capital to the housing market. The return of financial capital could be reasoned by China's economic slowing down and its rising labor cost. However, with no appropriate investment projects to absorb the returning overseas financial capital, possibly from wealthy entrepreneurs, the alternative was increased demand for high-end housing properties. According to Taiwan's official estimates, there was at least NT$10,000 billion (US$338 billion) of "idle capital" in the financial market (Chiang 2016). The question of how to convert "idle capital", generated mostly from rich entrepreneurs, from speculative investment to "real investment" is important not only for avoiding a potential financial crisis but also for a more equitable distribution of wealth.

In South Korea, housing sale prices have shown a clear rise since 2014. The rising demand for properties is attributed to the low interest rate, relaxation of housing finance rules, and rise in leasehold deposit prices. The speculative mood has been another driver for the housing prices. As a result, the transactions of apartment purchasing rights rose to 124,000 in September 2016, double the average transactions between 2012 and 2014. Despite the upsurge of housing prices in recent years, Korea's average housing prices are still below that in Canada, the US, Britain, and some big cities in China. While the overall property market is relatively stable in Korea, bubbles are forming in some areas such as the Gangnam district in Seoul, leading the government to take steps to curb overheating property markets in the capital city.

The financial burden following the growing housing price can be seen from the household expenditure by items. Taiwan's and South Korea's household expenditure by income quintile are shown in Tables 6.5 and 6.6. In Taiwan, housing, water, electricity, and other fuels accounted for the largest share of expenditure for the households in the lowest quintile (32 percent), followed by food (19 percent), health (17 percent), and recreation (13 percent). The expenditure share of housing, water, electricity, and other fuels declined with higher household income. For the households in the highest quintile, housing, water, electricity, and other fuels only accounted for 22 percent of total expenditure. In South Korea, it is food, beverages, and tobacco which accounted for the largest share of expenditure for the households in the lowest quintile (22 percent), followed by housing (17 percent), transport and communication (14 percent), and recreation, culture, restaurant, and hotels (14 percent). Similar to Taiwan, the expenditure share in housing, water, electricity, and other fuels also declined with higher household income. For households in the highest quintile in Korea, housing only accounted for 8 percent of their

Table 6.5 Taiwan's household expenditure by income quintile in 2015

	Lowest quintile	*Second quintile*	*Third quintile*	*Fourth quintile*	*Highest quintile*
Total consumption expenditure (NT dollar)	**339,536**	**544,624**	**723,571**	**921,454**	**1,269,049**
1. Food, beverages, and tobacco	19	18	17	16	14
2. Clothing and footwear	2	2	3	3	3
3. Housing, water, electricity, and other fuels	**32**	**29**	**25**	**23**	**22**
4. Furnishing, household equipment, and routine household maintenance	2	2	2	2	3
5. Health	17	16	15	15	14
6. Transport and communication	9	11	12	13	14
7. Recreation, culture, restaurant, and hotels	13	15	16	17	19
8. Education	1	3	4	5	5
9. Miscellaneous goods and services	4	5	5	6	6

Source: DGBAS (2016)

Table 6.6 South Korea's household expenditure by income quintile in 2014

	Lowest quintile	*Second quintile*	*Third quintile*	*Fourth quintile*	*Highest quintile*
Consumption expenditure (won)	**1,268,546**	**1,967,638**	**2,491,870**	**3,038,443**	**3,979,608**
1. Food, beverages, and tobacco	22	17	16	14	12
2. Clothing and footwear	5	6	6	6	7
3. Housing, water, electricity, and other fuels	**17**	**13**	**11**	**10**	**8**
4. Furnishing, household equipment, and routine household maintenance	4	4	4	4	5
5. Health	11	7	7	6	6
6. Transport and communication	14	17	18	18	18
7. Recreation, culture, restaurant, and hotels	14	19	19	20	21
8. Education	6	9	11	13	13
9. Miscellaneous goods and services	7	8	8	9	10

Source: KOSIS

expenditure. The expenditure on recreation, culture, restaurant, and hotels is the largest expenditure item (21 percent), followed by transport and communication (18 percent) and education (13 percent). Given the higher share of housing in the expenditure for the low-income family, the soaring prices for housing in recent years have added frost to snow for the lower income groups.

The financial burden from housing is an important reason for the rise of household debt in both countries. According to Fitch's estimate, Taiwan's household debt to GDP ratio was 82.6 percent in the first half of 2016 (Focus Taiwan News Channel May 20, 2017). South Korea's ratio was 91 percent at the end of 2015 (Yonhap News Agency April 6, 2017). Taiwan's and Korea's household debt to GDP ratios are higher than the average ratio (30 percent) of emerging countries and major developed countries, such as the US (78 percent), Japan (66 percent), France (56 percent), and Germany (54 percent) (Bank for International Settlement

2015). They are also far higher than the 66.4 percent recorded in Hong Kong and 41.8 percent in China. Since 2005, home mortgages have made up more than 50 percent of the total household debt in Taiwan with the ratio even hitting a high of 73 percent in 2010 (Focus Taiwan News Channel May 20, 2017). Several measures have been implemented to curb the rising housing prices. The most dramatic change has been the new property gains tax of as much as 45 percent which took effect on 1 January 2016. Despite the slowing down of housing prices, buying a home remains unaffordable for most young Taiwanese due to their low wages.

In South Korea, after the AFC, various factors have come together to contribute to the increase in household debt: the high commodity price level set by the government, the widespread use of credit cards to boost economic growth, the low interest policy that induced credit creation and the Korean financial institutions' shift of target customers from companies to individuals. The housing market boom in recent years further pushed up household debts. Up to June 2015, mortgage loans accounted for 44 percent of total household loans in all financial institutions in Korea. Non-bank financial institutions, which are less strictly regulated by the government than banks, took an important share in mortgages. At the end of Q1 2016, household loans made by banks totaled 569.3 trillion won (US$0.48 trillion), almost equaling the 589.1 trillion won (US$0.5 trillion) made by non-bank financial institutions (Chiang 2017). In 2011, the household debt for the lowest 20 percent of income earners was more than double of their annual income (Korea Institute for a New Society 2016).

A booming housing market benefits economic growth when exports and domestic industrial investment are sagging. However, household debt may result. Therefore, the quality of loans and greater growth of household income are essential to prevent a potential crisis from an overheated housing market. Any corresponding increase of interest rate on its part will add to the burden of households (especially the low-income ones) in their housing loan repayment. Private domestic consumption will be further constrained as a result. Ensuring low-income households have access to sufficient credit and financial services are also imperative to close the gap between the rich and the poor.

Conclusion

Taiwan and South Korea's Gini coefficient ratios are not high by international standards. However, the figures may not provide a real picture of the income inequality problem, given that many people in these two countries do feel the growing gap between the rich and the poor. According to the World Wealth and Income Database, the richest 1 percent of Taiwan's total population earned 11.3 percent of total fiscal income in 2012, increasing from 7.3 percent in 1995. In South Korea, the ratio increased from 6.9 percent to 12.2 percent during the same period. The top 10 percent of the population in Taiwan earned 36.4 percent of total fiscal income in 2013. In South Korea, the figure was more significant: 44.9 percent of fiscal income was earned by the top 10 percent of the population in 2012.

Several reasons could have contributed to the growing income inequality. First, while relocating factories to developing countries allowed companies in Taiwan and Korea to largely cut down their labor costs, the majority of domestic workers did not benefit from it. Many domestic workers had to shift to other positions in services with lower wages than they had been receiving while employed in the manufacturing sector. Otherwise they had to look for other job opportunities with better remuneration overseas. The second reason is the wage difference by company's size and by type of contract. This is particularly true for South Korea due to the immense differences between large profitable chaebols and SMEs. The massive layoffs and the "labor flexibility" policy after the AFC also caused an expansion of poorly paid non-regular workers in Korea. While contributing to the country's employment rate, these non-regular workers were paid less than regular workers and with less protection from social insurance. In 2017, non-regular contract employment still comprises a third of total employment in South Korea though the number has declined from its peak in the early 2000s. Third, business owners' wealth has been increasing, in contrast to employees' stagnant wages. The business owners' greater wealth is related to the relocation of manufacturing production abroad that allowed them to make greater profits. On the other hand, there are fewer opportunities with high remuneration for the workers with high education at home. Fourth, the escalating housing prices is another factor that worsens the income inequality. Despite the economic sluggishness, the housing market has been booming in Taiwan and Korea in recent years. The low interest rate is an important reason. Both the Taiwanese and Korean governments set a low interest rate as a way to stimulate the economic growth after the GFC. However, the low interest rate did not boost economic growth as much as expected. Instead, it encouraged more people to take mortgages from banks even though the housing price was high. The result is more household debt for the general public.

During the post-war industrialization period, the high economic growth rate in both countries made the income inequality less visible. However, with the economy slowing down, the unequal distribution of wealth has become a serious problem. Due to the weak external demand and growing competition from Chinese manufacturers, the Taiwanese and Korean economies are not going to enjoy high economic growth in the foreseeable future. In this "low economic growth" era, rising income inequality would only erode domestic consumption and even create conflict between different groups in societies. Income inequality would also make companies' profits unsustainable because of insufficient income to consume. This could become a vicious cycle that would lead the economy to downgrade even more.

References

Chiang, M.-H. (2016). *China-Taiwan Rapprochement: The political economy of cross-strait relations.* London and New York: Routledge.

Chiang, M.-H. (2017). *Contemporary South Korean economy: Challenges and prospects.* Singapore: World Scientific.

Delmendo, L. C. (2016, September). Taiwanese house prices continue to fall due to harsh taxes. Retrieved August 2, 2017, from https://www.globalpropertyguide.com/Asia/Taiwan/Price-History

Focus Taiwan News Channel. (2017, May 20). Household debt burden heavier than in China, Hong Kong. Retrieved July 27, 2017, from http://focustaiwan.tw/news/aeco/201705200006.aspx

Forbes. (2011, April 26). A Record Year. Retrieved October 29, 2014, from http://www.forbes.com/2011/04/26/korea-billionaires-11-lee-kun-hee-chung-mong-joon-introduction.html

Glyn, A. (2006). *Capitalism unleashed: Finance globalization and welfare.* New York: Oxford University Press.

Han, J., Liem, W.-s., & Lee, Y. (2013). In the Belly of the Beast: Samsung electronics' supply chain and work force in South Korea. Asia Monitor Resource Centre. Retrieved March 6, 2016, from http://old.amrc.org.hk/system/files/3%20Samsung%20Electronics%E2%80%99%20Supply%20Chain%20and%20Workforce%20in%20South%20Korea.pdf

Korea Institute for a New Society. (2016). *Angry figures: Report on the hidden inequality in South Korea.* Global Publishing Group (fen nu de shu zi: han guo yin cang de bu ping deng bao gao shu). Taipei: Global Publishing Group.

National Development Council (Taiwan). (2016). *Taiwan statistical data book 2016.* Taipei: Executive Yuan (Taiwan).

Nikkei Asian Review. (2014, April 10). Top four chaebol generate 90% of South Korean conglomerate profits. Retrieved January 15, 2015, from http://asia.nikkei.com/magazine/20140410-Growth-Central/Business/Top-four-chaebol-generate-90-of-South-Korean-conglomerate-profits

Noh, H.-G., Kim, H.-K., & Kim, Y.-G. (2014, July). Korea's rich people: Analysis on 2014 statistics. KB Research Report. Retrieved August 2, 2017, from http://www.koreafocus.or.kr/design2/layout/content_print.asp?group_id=105518

Randall, S. J., & Satoshi, U. (2013). *Labour market policies to promote growth and social cohesion in Korea*. OECD Economics Department Working Papers 1068. Paris: OECD Publishing.

Small and Medium Enterprise Administration (Taiwan). (1998). *White Paper on small and medium enterprises (zhong xiao qi ye bai pi shu)*. Taipei: Ministry of Economic Affairs (Taiwan).

Small and Medium Enterprise Administration (Taiwan). (2006). *White Paper on small and medium enterprises (zhong xiao qi ye bai pi shu)*. Taipei: Ministry of Economic Affairs (Taiwan).

Small and Medium Enterprise Administration (Taiwan). (2016). *White Paper on small and medium enterprises (zhong xiao qi ye bai pi shu)*. Taipei: Ministry of Economic Affairs (Taiwan).

The Reporter. (2016, August 6). The real truth behind Taiwan's income gap. Retrieved March 2, 2017, from https://www.twreporter.org/a/taiwan-wealth-inequality

The World Bank. (2016). Measuring inequality. Retrieved June 27, 2017, from http://web.worldbank.org/WBSITE/EXTERNAL/TOPICS/EXTPOVERTY/EXTPA/0,,contentMDK:20238991~menuPK:435055~pagePK:148956~piPK:216618~theSitePK:430367,00.html

Yonhap News Agency. (2014, July 8). 17 S. Korean firms make Fortune 500 list. Retrieved January 15, 2015, from http://english.yonhapnews.co.kr/business/2014/07/08/44/0501000000AEN20140708008800320F.html

Yonhap News Agency. (2017, April 6). Ratio of S. Korea's household debt to GDP is higher than OECD average. Retrieved July 27, 2017, from http://english.yonhapnews.co.kr/news/2017/04/06/0200000000AEN20170406007700320.html

CHAPTER 7

New Challenges Ahead (II): Aging Population

Abstract Like Japan, Taiwan, and South Korea are facing potential challenges from the aging population. The statistics from the UN showed that in 2030, over one-third of population will be aged 60 and above in both countries. The economy could be slowing down even further due to the lower propensity to consume. On the other hand, the government expenditure could be increased in order to fulfill the demand from the greater number of senior citizens. At present, the government debts to GDP ratios are low in both countries. The governments' financial burden could become a challenge in the future if the economy continued to remain fragile. Policy reforms that incorporate comprehensive social welfare and sustainable economic development are therefore imperative.

Keywords Aging population • Total fertility rate • Dependency ratio • Female labor participation • Social welfare policy

With rising life expectancy and plummeting birthrates, both Taiwan and South Korea are about to undergo a stunning demographic transformation. Taiwan is set to become a "super-aged" society in 2025 with more than 20 percent of the population aged 65 and above. South Korea will follow suit in 2030. The falling total fertility rate (TFR) and rising longevity are the two fundamental contributors to the growing aging population. The economic growth prospect may take a beating as savings,

M.-H. Chiang, *Post-Industrial Development in East Asia*,
https://doi.org/10.1007/978-981-13-0274-9_7

consumption, and investment are expected to decline subsequent to the aging demography. More importantly, an aging population means a smaller workforce and therefore less tax revenue for the government to support the unemployed elderly. Several policy measures have been initiated to tackle the potential impact of aging population on the economy. Still, the low TFR shows that policy aimed at encouraging birth has not been very effective.

The purpose of this chapter is to investigate the development of demography in Taiwan and South Korea over the last few decades and to analyze the potential consequences of an aging population on their future economic development. It is organized as follows. The first section compares Taiwan's and South Korea's demographic statistics with other countries. At present, the two countries' demographic structure is still relatively young compared to other developed countries. Nonetheless, the continuous low TFR will lead Taiwan and South Korea toward becoming aging societies in the next decades. The second section explores the development of population by age groups in both countries from the 1960s to present. One of the most obvious impacts following an aging population is the change to labor structure. The pool of young workers shrinks while the middle- to old-aged workers become the majority in the labor market. As such, the third section assesses the transformation of labor force by different age groups. Several measures are proposed in order to minimize the impact from the declining number of young laborers. Fourth, due to the inadequate social welfare policy, the growing aged population with insufficient disposable income has become a social problem. The elderly's financial vulnerability and the government's social expenditure are discussed.

Taiwan's and South Korea's "Demographic Time Bomb"

An aging population is a general phenomenon that most developed countries are experiencing. However, the aging population statistics from the UN shows that Taiwan and South Korea will be seriously hit by problems from an aging population. As shown in Table 7.1, in 2015, 18.6 percent of the total population in Taiwan was aged 60 years and above, while in South Korea, the ratio was 18.5 percent. These ratios are still far beneath that of Japan and some European countries. However, the aging population is expected to grow very quickly in the coming decades. In 2030, the

Table 7.1 International ranking of estimated percentage of population aged 60 and over in 2015, 2030, and 2050

2015		*2030*		*2050*	
Country ranking	*Percentage*	*Country ranking*	*Percentage*	*Country ranking*	*Percentage*
1 Japan	33.1	2 Japan	37.3	**1 Taiwan**	**44.3**
2 Italy	28.6	3 Italy	36.6	2 Japan	42.5
3 Germany	27.6	4 Germany	36.1	**3 South Korea**	**41.5**
4 Finland	27.2	5 Portugal	34.7	4 Spain	41.4
5 Portugal	27.1	14 Finland	31.5	5 Portugal	41.2
52 Taiwan	**18.6**	**15 South Korea**	**31.4**	8 Italy	40.7
53 South Korea	**18.5**	**16 Taiwan**	**31.3**	13 Germany	39.3

Source: United Nations (2015)

population aged 60 and over will account for 31.3 percent and 31.4 percent of the total populations in Taiwan and South Korea respectively. According to the UN's estimates, in 2050, Taiwan's ratio will increase to 44.3 percent, making it the oldest country in the world. South Korea's ratio will also expand to 41.5 percent, ranking it third, after Taiwan and Japan. The UN's forecast also showed that the number of the elderly (aged 60 and above) in Taiwan will increase from the current 4.4 million in 2015 to 7.2 million in 2030 and 9.2 million in 2050. The number for South Korea will increase from 9.3 million in 2015 to 21 million in 2030 (United Nations 2015).

Falling TFR and rising longevity are the two fundamental contributors to the growing aging population. The average TFR in Taiwan and South Korea were 1.1 and 1.3 respectively between 2010 and 2015, far below the global average (2.5) (Table 7.2). The asymmetry is in the rapidly declining TFR and longer life expectancy. The life expectancy at birth in both countries is higher than the global average and equivalent to the high-income countries. The life expectancy at birth for males in Taiwan was 74.6 and 82.3 for females during the 2010–2015 period. In South Korea, the ratios were 78 and 84.6 respectively. As a result of low TFR and longevity, the dependency ratio (measured by people aged 65 and over per 100 people aged 20–64) is expected to increase from 47.6 percent in 2015 to 64.6 percent in 2030 in Taiwan. As for Korea, the ratio will increase from 50.6 percent to 70.4 percent.

Table 7.2 Demographic statistics in Taiwan, South Korea, and the world

	Total fertility rate (number of children per woman, 2010–2015)	*Life expectancy at birth (2010–2015)*		*Total dependency ratio (%)*		*Labor force participation of persons aged 65 or over (2015) (%)*	
		Male	*female*	*2015*	*2030*	*Male*	*female*
Taiwan	**1.1**	**74.6**	**82.3**	**47.6**	**64.6**	n/a	n/a
South Korea	**1.3**	**78.0**	**84.6**	**50.6**	**70.4**	**42.2**	**23.4**
High-income countries	1.7	75.7	81.9	64.8	78.0	18.2	9.8
Middle-income countries	2.4	67.7	71.5	70.8	71.0	35.3	15.9
Low-income countries	4.9	58.7	61.9	131.1	110.5	n/a	n/a
World average	2.5	68.3	72.7	73.5	75.7	30.2	14.4

Source: United Nations (2015)

One thing worth noticing in Table 7.2 is the high percentage of senior employment in South Korea. In 2015, 42.2 percent of Korean males aged 65 and above were still working. For the Korean females, the ratio was 23.4 percent. An important reason for this is the inadequate social welfare system for supporting the living expenses of the elderly. In 2014, 55 percent of the elderly aged 55–70 (about 6 million people) had neither private nor public pensions to finance their daily necessities while the remaining 45 percent received an average pension of 490,000 won (about US$411.8) per month.

Evolution of Taiwan's and South Korea's Demographic Changes

In 1965, more than half of the total populations in Taiwan and South Korea were still under 19 years (Tables 7.3 and 7.4). After the 1970s, the age structure started to change dramatically. In Taiwan, the share of a youth population under age 19 years declined from 47.2 percent in 1975 to 20 percent by 2015. The people aged between 20 and 39 years had no significant changes during the same period whereas people in the middle range (40–59 years old) increased from 17.5 percent to 30.8 percent. The aging population (60 and above) increased from 4.5 percent in 1965 to 19 percent in 2015. A similar development of aging population can be

Table 7.3 Taiwan's population by age group 1965–2015

	0–19	*20–39*	*40–59*	*60–79*	*80 and above*	*Total population (million people)*
1965	54.4	25.9	15.2	4.5		12.6
1975	47.2	29.3	17.5	5.6	0.3	16.2
1985	39.5	35.1	17.3	7.6	0.6	19.3
1995	33.2	35.0	20.8	9.9	1.1	21.4
2005	25.7	33.0	28.1	11.3	1.9	22.8
2015	20.0	30.3	30.8	15.9	3.1	23.5

Source: Department of statistics, Ministry of the Interior (2016); National Development Council (Taiwan) (2012)
As % of total population

Table 7.4 South Korea's population by age group 1965–2015

	0–19	*20–39*	*40–59*	*60–79*	*80 and above*	*Total population (million people)*
1965	52.9	28.1	14.1	4.6	0.3	28.7
1975	50.9	28.5	15.1	5.1	0.4	35.3
1985	41.0	34.3	18.0	6.2	0.5	40.8
1995	32.0	37.9	20.9	8.3	0.8	45.1
2005	25.7	33.5	27.7	11.7	1.4	48.1
2015	20.2	28.6	32.8	15.7	2.8	50.6

Source: CEIC (2017)
As % of total population

observed in South Korea. The youth population under age 19 years declined from 50.9 percent of the total population in 1975 to 20.2 percent by 2015. During the same period, the population aged between 40 and 59 years increased from 14.1 percent to 32.8 percent while the elderly aged 60 years and above increased from 5.5 percent to 18.5 percent.

How did Taiwan and South Korea become the aging societies that they are today? Government policy to decelerate population growth is often an important reason for the declining share of young people in a population and growing importance of the elderly. The rapid population growth after WWII was considered a hindrance to economic development. To reduce the economic burden, the Taiwanese government started its "family planning policy" in 1964. Each family was encouraged to have only two children (National Archives Administration 2015). Similarly, as part of the

Korean government's economic development policies, the national family planning campaign to limit births began in 1962. To further increase per capita living standard, the Park Chung-hee administration set out policies to reduce population growth, from a three-child family in 1968 to two-child family in 1971 and one or two-child(ren) in the early 1980s (Howe et al. 2007). With the policy initiatives, Taiwan's total fertility rates declined quickly from 7 in 1951 to 5.6 in 1961 and 3.7 in 1971 (Data source: Ministry of Interior). Taiwan's birth rates, measured by the total number of newborn babies per 1000 persons in a year also dropped visibly from 23 in 1981 to 16 in 1991, 12 in 2001, and 8.5 in 2015. In South Korea, the birth rates declined from 44 in 1960 to 31 in 1970, 23 in 1980, and 15 in 1990. After the 2000s, the birth rate continued to fall to 8.6 in 2015 (Data source: Korean statistical information services). Beyond the policy measures, the quick economic development was accompanied by the social trend of late marriages and childbearing. The high cost of education and living also discouraged people from having children.

The rapid slowing down of the birth rate took place alongside a steady decline of the death rate. The improved public health measures and medical advances following economic development explain the decreasing mortality rates. In Taiwan, the annual death rate decreased from 9 per 1000 people in 1950 to 7 in 2015 (Data source: Ministry of Interior). In South Korea, the annual death rate dropped from 14 deaths per 1000 people in 1960 to 5 in 2015 (Data source: Korean statistical information services).

Amid growing concern that a rapidly aging society and labor shortage would result in mounting social challenges, the Taiwanese government revised its Guidelines for Population Policy as early as in 1992 in a bid to maintain reasonable population growth. In the following years, the government introduced various pro-natal measures, such as financial assistance for dependent children, special tax rebates, paid maternity leave, and so on. The Gender Equality of Employment Law was enacted in 2002 in order to prevent discrimination toward married and pregnant female workers. The Ministry of Interior (MOI) in 2008 introduced further steps to encourage firms and businesses to adopt family-friendly workplace practices as well as child-safe environments. Policymakers hoped these measures would motivate working females to have children and help lift the overall fertility rate. Similarly, the Korean government implemented several policies to deal with the aging challenges more than a decade ago. In 2005, an advisory committee to South Korea's president was formed and a law was passed to offer a legal framework to promote birth rates. The Saero-Maji Plan for the 2006–2010 period included measures to construct a favorable environment for childbearing. In 2006, the government announced "Vision 2020 Plan" to raise the TFR (Haub 2010). However, the policy initiatives have not been able to effectively boost Taiwan's and South Korea's TFR, which remain among the lowest in the world. The governments may have to rely on other labor policies to complement the current TFP promotion policy, including the reduction of working hours and encouraging men to take leave to share the childcare burden and so on. Moreover, once the policies have been initiated, the execution also matters. At present, both societies may not be fully aware of the significance of a shrinking youth population.

Aging Population Leads to Changes in Labor Force Structure

The aging population has affected the structure of the labor force in Taiwan and South Korea. The youth labor force has been declining whereas the number of senior workers has been rising. As shown in Table 7.5, in 2000, Taiwanese workers aged between 15 and 29 years old accounted for 27.6 percent of the total labor force. This ratio declined to 19.8 percent by 2015. During the same period, the share of workers aged between 30 and 44 also decreased from 45.1 percent to 41.5 percent. On the other hand, the share of Taiwan workers aged between 45 and 59 in the total labor force expanded from 23 percent in 2000 to 31.9 percent by 2015. The share of Taiwan workers above 60 years old increased from 4.2

Table 7.5 Taiwan and South Korea's labor force by age group in 2000 and 2015

	Taiwan		*South Korea*	
	2000	*2015*	*2000*	*2015*
15–29	27.6	19.8	24.0	16.1
30–44	45.1	41.5	43.1	34.3
45–59	23.0	31.9	23.9	35.7
60 and above	4.2	6.7	9.0	14.0
Total labor force (million people)	9.8	11.6	22.1	26.9

Source: CEIC (2017), National Statistics (2017)
Unit: As % of total labor force

percent to 6.7 percent during the same period. A similar trend of declining youth labor force and growing number of senior workers can be found in South Korea. One thing worth noticing is that Korea has a greater share of laborers aged 60 and above. The percentage was 9 percent in 2000 and increased to 14 percent by 2015. This is more than double of Taiwan's ratio.

With the aging population, the young labor force is expected to shrink sharply in the following decades. According to Taiwan's official estimates, the working population has already begun to decline since 2015. In 2060, the working population aged between 15 and 64 years is estimated to be around 1 million, declining from 17 million in 2016. Nearly half of them will be aged between 45 and 64 years (National Development Council 2016). South Korea is also expected to experience a similar shrinking working population. OECD estimated that over the period 2020–2050, the growth of workers in South Korea will become negative and experience a sharp drop (Phang 2005).

Even though the policy measures to encourage women to give birth could be effective, it would take at least two decades to see an increase in the working population. At present, two principal measures could counterbalance the potential impact on the economy from the shrinking working population. First is to increase the labor productivity. Since the economically active population will continue to age and decrease in number, labor productivity must be enhanced in order to maintain a decent level of economic growth. Compared with most of the advanced countries, the labor productivity in Taiwan and South Korea still has much room for improvement. As shown in Table 7.6, in 2014, Taiwan's productivity in all sectors was US$18.9 per hour worked, lower than South Korea's US$31.2 and the OECD countries' average of US$45.9. Comparing Taiwan's and South Korea's labor productivity in the manufacturing sector, Taiwan's labor productivity (US$9.5) was much lower than that of South Korea. In services, the average monthly wage in Taiwan is NT$48,490 (about US$1616), lower than South Korea's 3,300,100 won (about US$2908). However, the labor productivity measured by output per hour worked may not be very accurate. In the case of Taiwan, the laborers' wages have been depressed for many years. Taiwan might have produced similar value of goods and services as South Korea but the understated wages do not really reflect the real production value. The labor productivity index compiled by Taiwan's government showed that Taiwan's labor productivity in the manufacturing sector progressed from

Table 7.6 Labor statistics in Taiwan, South Korea and OECD average

	Taiwan	*South Korea*	*OECD average*
	2015	*2014*	*2014*
1. Productivity (US$ per hour worked)	18.9	31.2	45.9
2. Productivity in manufacturing sectors (US$ per hour worked)	9.5	22.5 (2015)	n/a
3. Productivity in service sectors (monthly wage NT$ and Korean won)	48,490	3,300,100	n/a
3. Female labor force participation rate by age group (%)			
25–29	90	73	72
30–34	82	60	71
35–39	**75**	**57**	**72**
40–44	**76**	**64**	**73**
45–49	70	70	74
50–54	57	66	71
55–59	40	58	62
4. Elderly labor force participation rate by age group (%)			
65 and above	8.8	31	n/a
65–69	n/a	46	25
70–74	n/a	34	15
5. Unemployment rate by age group (%)			
15–24	11	10	15
25–34	5	6	9
35–44	3	2	6
45–54	2	2	6

Source: OECD (2017), Ministry of Labor (2017), National Statistics (2017)

100 in 2011 to 102.5 in 2015. In comparison, South Korea's labor productivity in manufacturing sectors declined from 100 in 2010 to 95.8 in 2015 (National Statistics, 2016).

When comparing productivity in different sectors within each country, the gap is less obvious in Taiwan. Taiwan's labor productivity in services in 2014 was 82 percent of that in the manufacturing sector. On the other hand, OECD's figures showed that South Korea's productivity in services in 2012 was only about 45 percent of that in its manufacturing sector, far below OECD countries' average of 86 percent (OECD 2014). South Korea's low productivity in services can be attributed to the export-led growth strategy after the war which has attracted the most productive resources into large manufacturing giants, instead of the large number of SMEs in services.

Second is the quantitative expansion of the labor force through encouraging the labor participation of women, the elderly, and the youth in the labor force. As shown in Table 7.6, the youth female labor participation rate in South Korea aged between 25 and 44 years is relatively low compared to Taiwan. In particular, for the Korean female aged between 30 and 44 years, labor participation rate is even lower than OCED's average. This shows that the childrearing responsibility is still on women when they start a family in South Korea. It is also difficult for Korean females to find proper jobs after leaving work for several years. The wage dispersion may have also discouraged women participation in the workforce in South Korea after marriage. In 2011, female employees in South Korea were paid only 64 percent of the wages of male employees, the largest gap among OECD countries (OECD 2014). After the age of 45, the female labor participation in Korea began to increase. For Korean women aged between 50 and 54 years, the labor participation rate was 66 percent compared to 57 percent in Taiwan. For women aged between 55 and 59 years, the rate declined to 58 percent but it is still higher than Taiwan's 40 percent.

In contrast with the low rate of female labor participation, the elderly constitutes a strong labor force in South Korea. Participation rate for those aged between 70 and 74 had clear growth from 27 percent in 2000 to 34 percent by 2014, double that of OECD countries' average of 15 percent. In comparison, the elderly's labor force participation rate in Taiwan was low (8.8 percent).

The youth female labor participation rate is high in Korea but the overall unemployment rate for youths remains high. Taiwan also has a similar high unemployment rate for its youths. As exhibited in Table 7.6, the unemployment rate for youths aged 15 and 24 years was over 10 percent in both countries. The reason is disequilibrium in supply and demand in the jobs market. As previously mentioned, the slow progress of industrial upgrading cannot keep up with demand from the large number of highly educated youth who look for high-value-added jobs. In South Korea, due to the wage differences between chaebols and SMEs, many young Korean people would rather stay unemployed until they manage to find a job in large firms.

Beyond domestic laborers, foreign workers could be an immediate solution to Taiwan's and South Korea's declining labor forces. Until the end of 2016, there were nearly 624,768 foreign labors in Taiwan. Among them, 243,000 were foreign laborers working in industries and 203,000 were domestic helpers and care workers. The majority of foreign laborers came from Southeast Asia (Data source: Ministry of Labor). In June 2016, Taiwan passed an amendment to the Employment Service Act to make it easier for qualified foreign laborers to stay on without having to apply for new work visas. This is one of several measures—including a proposal to attract and/or retain foreign students and overseas talent—undertaken by the government in a bid to stem the "brain drain" after many Taiwanese professionals chose to relocate overseas in search of better employment opportunities. Likewise, in 2015, there were around 0.94 million foreign workers in South Korea, 91 percent of whom came from Asia (Data source: KOSIS).

The Elderly's Financial Vulnerabilities

Table 7.7 shows the household income and expenditure for the lowest 20th percentile income group in Taiwan. Households with their oldest member aged 65 and above accounted for the largest number (880,962 households or 52.5 percent of total age groups). Their disposable income is the lowest among all age groups (NT$298,817). This amount of disposable income is not sufficient to cover basic consumption expenditure. In comparison, households comprising young families with household heads aged below 39 years accounted for less than 10 percent of total low-income groups. Another way to look at the elderly's poverty problem is through the comparison of head of household aged 65 and above in all income groups. A total of 53.4 percent of them are in the lowest income

Table 7.7 Taiwan's average family income and consumption for household in the lowest income quantile by age of household head in 2015

	No. of households	*As % of total household*	*Average no. of persons*	*Disposable income (NT$)*	*Consumption expenditure (NT$)*
Under 30 years	44,388	2.6	1.9	400,789	439,193
30–34	42,341	2.5	1.9	372,421	357,351
35–39	68,378	4.1	2.1	380,332	387,651
40–44	64,503	3.8	2.0	365,090	358,410
45–54	202,386	12.1	1.8	343,182	359,438
55–64	374,342	22.3	1.7	324,417	353,293
65 and above	880,962	52.5	1.6	298,817	318,125

Source: DGBAS (2016)

Table 7.8 South Korea's average income and expenditure by household head's age in 2015

	Average age of household head	*As % of total household*	*Average no. of persons*	*Income (won)*	*Expenditure (won)*
Under 39 years	34.8	21.2	3.3	4,456,397	3,361,819
40–49	44.5	31.4	3.6	5,005,338	4,028,139
50–59	54.3	23.9	3.0	5,137,197	3,815,819
60 and above	69.0	25.7	2.4	3,004,092	2,252,020

Source: KOSIS (2017)

groups, followed by 22.7 percent in the second lowest income group and only 13 percent of them are in the highest two income groups. In other words, over half of Taiwan's aged persons (by age of household head) are in the lowest income group. A similar trend of a poor and aging population can be found in South Korea. As shown in Table 7.8, the households with their eldest member being aged 60 and above accounted for 25.7 percent of total households. Their income and expenditure are the lowest among all age groups.

Financial vulnerability of the elderly is probably a more serious problem in South Korea than in Taiwan. The lack of financial resources explains the higher labor participation rate for the elderly in Korea. In fact, traditionally, as Confucian societies, the elderly in Taiwan and South Korean have relied on younger family members for financial support. However, with the rise of "individualism" or "Western values", more and more South Koreans are convinced that their parents should support themselves. According to the Asian Development Bank, around 20 percent of the elderly's living expenses are financed by family members in South Korea, lower than the 45 percent in Taiwan and 33 percent in Thailand (Lee and Mason 2011). This explains why the suicide rate among elderly South Koreans is by far the highest in the country and in the world. In 2013, the suicide rate in South Korea was 64.2 per 100,000 people for those aged 65 and above. This ratio is significantly higher than the average suicide rate in the country (28.5 per 100,000 people) (Statistics Korea 2015). The average suicide rate in OECD countries was 12 for every 100,000 people. The 2014 official survey pointed out that economic difficulties were the principal reason for suicide (40.4%) of the elderly, followed by health reasons (24.4%), loneliness (13.3%), conflicts with family and friends (11.5%), family and friends' death, health problems, and others (10.4%).

Financing the "Super-Aged" Societies

From 1949 to the mid-1970s, very limited social welfare programs were enacted in Taiwan. Social welfare was seen as burdensome to economic growth. Most assistance was targeted at a few exclusive groups, such as military personnel and their dependents, government employees, and teachers. Social-assistance programs were only targeted at very low-income families (Huang and Ku 2011). The social insurance scheme, introduced in the 1950s, included insurances for soldiers, laborers, and government employees (Tang 2000, p. 72). After the democratization in the 1980s, Taiwan's social policy was profoundly altered. There were more voices and concerns for the poor population's social welfare from the opposition parties. In response to popular demand, political candidates campaigned for more social welfare legislation and extensive social welfare coverage to young and old, women, and disadvantaged ethnic groups (Tsai, 2002, pp. 372–373). In addition, when Taiwan became more and more isolated in the international arena with the withdrawal from the UN in the late 1970s, the KMT government realized that it had to build stronger domestic support to justify its political legitimacy. The ruling KMT government had to extend its welfare concessions to a wider public in order to gain popular support and electoral success (Tang, 2000, p. 64). The implementation of the National Health Insurance (NHI) in 1995 was the milestone in Taiwan's advancement in social welfare policy. The NHI is a universal health coverage scheme that provides comprehensive health insurance to Taiwan citizens as well as foreign residents. With the implementation of the NHI, the social welfare expenditure clearly increased from NT$96,207 million in 1990 to NT$231,766 million by 1995 and doubled to NT$531,809 million by 2000 (National Development Council 2016, p. 180). The NHI not only affords equity but also augments social solidarity by providing subsidies for premiums and medical services to the poor and disadvantaged populations (Cheng 2015). Unlike the KMT's economy-first policy, the DPP was known for its pro-welfare ideology. However, soon after Chen Shui-bian took office in 2000, the DPP government abandoned its ideas of social welfare due to controversies over the government's potential insolvency and a national pension scheme (Huang and Ku 2011). The DPP government's hesitance and eventual abandonment of extensive social welfare spending can be observed from the figures. As indicated in Table 7.9, Taiwan's social welfare spending declined from 2001 onward, after its peak in 2000. From 2001 to 2009,

Table 7.9 Social welfare spending in Taiwan and South Korea 1995–2015

	Social welfare spending (NT$ million and million won)		*Social welfare spending (as % of GDP)*	
	Taiwan	*South Korea*	*Taiwan*	*South Korea*
1995	231,766	14,860,337	12.1	3.5
1996	290,002	17,471,493	15.7	3.6
1997	294,982	21,460,628	15.7	4.1
1998	282,767	30,806,632	14.2	5.9
1999	280,452	37,208,202	13.7	6.5
2000	531,809	34,013,069	16.9	5.4
2001	396,981	38,415,580	17.5	5.6
2002	323,615	40,889,420	15.1	5.4
2003	346,911	46,210,661	15.7	5.7
2004	347,557	55,767,735	15.5	6.4
2005	357,762	62,092,037	15.6	6.8
2006	370,303	73,566,452	16.7	7.6
2007	372,202	80,619,610	16.3	7.7
2008	368,136	91,103,439	15.7	8.3
2009	388,562	105,933,317	14.5	9.2
2010	415,356	112,125,400	16.2	8.9
2011	446,922	117,636,239	17.1	8.8
2012	540,440	130,072,556	20.2	9.4
2013	536,912	143,052,704	20.1	10.0
2014	517,143	156,245,613	19.5	10.5
2015	532,100	n/a	20.1	n/a

Source: DGBAS; National Development Council (2016), KOSIS (2017)

Taiwan's social welfare expenditure ranged between NT$323,651 million and NT$396,981 million. It peaked to NT$540,440 million in 2012 when Ma Ying-jeou, from the KMT, was in office. In terms of the share of social welfare spending in GDP, it was maintained at 15–17 percent from 2001 to 2011 before it jumped to over 20 percent in 2013.

The development of social welfare expenditure in Taiwan has been driven by social insurance. As shown in Table 7.10, social insurance took up 53.5 percent of total social welfare expenditure in 1995. The ratio increased to 67.4 percent in 2015. During the same period, the shares of other items such as social assistance, welfare services, employment, and health insurance all declined. Social insurance includes insurance for public servants, laborers, employees, farmers, and life insurance. Public

Table 7.10 Taiwan's social welfare expenditure by items 1995–2015

	1995	*2000*	*2005*	*2010*	*2011*	*2012*	*2013*	*2014*	*2015*
Social insurance	53.4	53.4	52.8	58.8	60.0	64.3	67.8	65.6	67.4
Social assistance	5.3	5.2	2.6	3.4	3.3	2.7	2.5	2.4	2.1
Welfare services	33.8	35.2	38.9	30.5	30.0	27.9	24.9	27.0	26.0
Employment	1.6	0.7	0.7	0.6	0.8	0.6	0.5	0.5	0.4
Health insurance	6.0	5.5	5.0	6.7	6.0	4.6	4.3	4.6	4.2

Source: National Statistics (2017)
As % of total social welfare expenditure

servants and military personnel in Taiwan have been the main recipients of social insurance. Their premium per insurant is much higher than other laborers and employees in private firms. Although Taiwan's fiscal position is good, the growing demand for pensions as the population ages raises questions over whether it is sustainable in the long run. The shrinking working-age population will mean less tax revenue, while the growing elderly population will place more demands on the pension and healthcare systems. As such, the new DPP government led by Tsai Ing-wen has initiated reforms over the national pension system since 2016 to equalize income distribution and to relieve future fiscal pressure.

South Korea's social security provisions began in the 1960s under the Park Chung-hee administration. The primary purpose was to win popular support for the military regime (Tang, 2000, p. 93). As economic development was the priority for the government, social policy became subordinated to the state's economic development policy. Hence, the institutions in charge of social policies were underdeveloped during the authoritarian period. Korea's democratization in the 1980s allowed more interest groups to play a central role in directing the development of social welfare policies. After the AFC, the policymakers were conceived that one of the ways to improve economic conditions was to consolidate and expand the welfare policies. The high figures in unemployment also drove home the importance of insurance to the public, as a safety net in case of any unpredicted crisis. The election of Kim Dae-jung saw a deep rupture with the previous administration with regard to social policy. Kim pursued comprehensive, instead of incremental reforms (Fiori and Kim 2011). The introduction of the National Basic Livelihood Security (NBLS) is often referred to as the most representative of all social welfare reforms under the Kim administration. The Bill was enacted in 2000. Anyone with income and assets below a certain level was eligible for social assistance. Moreover, the NHI underwent significant changes. In spite of some opposition, all health insurance systems were merged into one single national insurer that aimed to improve equality in health insurance contributions among the insured through a united nationwide contribution system (Fiori and Kim 2011).

The development of social welfare policies has resulted in a clear growth of social welfare spending from 14,860,337 million won in 1995 to 30,806,632 million won in 1998 (Table 7.9). Unlike Taiwan's stagnation of social welfare expenditure in the 2000s, Korea's social welfare spending continued to grow throughout the 2000s. The social welfare spending in Korea's GDP was however less than Taiwan's ratio. South Korea's greater economic size may explain its relatively small share of social welfare expenditure in GDP. After the GFC, South Korea's social welfare expenditure as percentage of GDP increased to 9.2 percent in 2009. It continued to progress to 10.5 percent in 2014. As shown in Table 7.11, the social welfare expenditure is mainly on old-aged persons and health which accounted for 28.8 percent and 38 percent respectively of total social welfare expenditure in 2014. In the same table, "family", "active labor market programs", and "unemployment" are the three items that have seen a robust growth in terms of share in social welfare expenditure. The share of social welfare expenditure in "family" increased from 1.8 percent in 1995 to 11 percent by 2014. During the same period, the share in "active labor market programs" and "unemployment" also enlarged to 4.3 percent and 2.7 percent respectively, from

Table 7.11 South Korea's social welfare expenditure by items 1995–2014

	1995	*2000*	*2005*	*2010*	*2011*	*2012*	*2013*	*2014*
Old age	36.1	32.5	24.7	25.5	26.1	27.4	26.9	28.8
Survivors	4.3	3.2	3.2	2.9	3.0	2.9	2.5	2.5
Incapacity-related benefits	11.7	8.5	10.0	7.2	7.6	7.7	7.1	6.7
Health	41.9	40.3	42.6	42.7	42.8	40.0	38.5	38.0
Family	1.8	2.6	3.9	8.1	8.1	9.3	11.9	11.0
Active labor market programs	1.1	6.8	1.6	3.6	3.3	4.0	4.4	4.3
Unemployment	0.0	1.4	2.8	3.3	3.0	2.8	2.7	2.7
Others	3.1	4.8	11.0	6.6	6.0	5.9	6.0	6.0

As% of total social welfare expenditure
Source: KOSIS (2017)

1.1 percent and 0 percent. The growing shares in the above three items showed the increase in financial aid transferred to promote the birth rate and alleviate unemployment problems.

Conclusion

The development of Taiwan's and South Korea's aging population is quite similar. During the 1960s and 1970s, both governments appealed for birth control measures through a voluntary family planning program, owing to fears of adverse consequences from rapid population growth on the economy. The birth control led to a sharp decline in TFR during the 1980s. Meanwhile, with the advancement of medical technology and life quality, life expectancy has increased. As a consequence, the share of senior workers in total domestic employment has increased whereas the share of youth labor has dipped. The aging demographic challenge could put the brakes on the country's economic development in the future.

In theory, a smaller pool of laborers will result in less production in an economy. The government will have less tax revenue from the producers. At the same time, the growing aging population means there is increasing welfare expenditure required from the government. With the limited growth of the youth population, maintaining moderate economic growth to support an expanding welfare program will be a big challenge for the government. Although both the Taiwanese and South Korean governments are in good financial health, the economic slowing down as a result of aging population could eventually render the governments' social welfare expenditure unsustainable. So far, the policy measures to encourage women to give birth have not been effective. This can be seen from the still low TFR ratios in both countries. Successful increase in labor participation of women and young people may alleviate the impact from the declining number of laborers, given that the unemployment rates for these two groups in both countries are relatively higher compared to other age groups. The labor participation rate for women is particularly low in South Korea. Introducing foreign workers may also help to make up the shortfall in the shrinking labor force. Nevertheless, like in other migrant societies, social integration between domestic and foreign workers will be a concern. In the long run, the young immigrants would also age. As such, domestic adjustment in education, economy, and social policy will probably be a more sustainable solution. Indeed, the ineffective policy encouragement for women to give birth shows that the social policy (i.e., subsidies and more maternity leave) is not the key. Other measures such as more flexible employment and flexible working days for married couples, affordable public housing, gender equality, and so on are also important to construct a friendly environment for childrearing. Finally, increasing productivity through automation may also help. More sophisticated technology can be expected to complement the shortage of labor, for instance, robotic devices in households may be helpful to ease the burden of elderly care and boost the female labor participation rate.

References

CEIC Global Database (2017). Retrieved September 28, 2017, from https://www.ceicdata.com/zh-hans

Cheng, Tsung-Mei. (2015). Taiwan's health care system: The Next 20 Years. Taiwan-US Quarterly Analysis, The Brookings Institution. Retrieved March 4, 2017, from https://www.brookings.edu/opinions/taiwans-health-care-system-the-next-20-years

Department of statistics, Ministry of the Interior (Taiwan). (2016). Population by single year of age.

Directorate-General of Budget, Accounting and Statistics (DGBAS). 2016. Report on the survey of family income and expenditure, 2015 (jia ting shou zhi diao cha bao gao). Executive Yuan, Taiwan. Retrieved August 16, 2017, from http://win.dgbas.gov.tw/fies/doc/result/104.pdf

Fiori, A., & Kim, S. (2011). The dynamics of welfare policy-making in South Korea: Social movements as policy entrepreneurs. *Asian Social Work and Policy Review*, *5*(2), 61–78.

Haub, Carl. (2010). Did South Korea's population policy work too well? Population Reference Bureau. Retrieved August 17, 2017, from http://www.prb.org/Publications/Articles/2010/koreafertility.aspx

Howe, N., Jackson, R., & Nakashima K. (2007). *The ageing of Korea*. Centre for Strategic and International Studies. Retrieved March 28, 2016, from http://csis.org/files/media/csis/pubs/070321_gai_agingkorea_eng.pdf

Huang, C.-C., & Ku, Y.-w. (2011). Effectiveness of social welfare programmes in East Asia: A case study of Taiwan. *Social Policy & Administration, 45*(7), 733–751.

Korean Statistical Information Service (KOSIS). (2017). Statistics Korea. Retrieved March 2, 2018, from http://kosis.kr/eng/

Lee, Sang-Hyop and Mason, Andrew (2011). The Economic Life Cycle and Support Systems in Asia. No. 283. Manila: Asian Development Bank. Retrieved

March 5, 2018, from https://www.adb.org/sites/default/files/publication/30453/economics-wp283.pdf

Ministry of labor (Taiwan). (2017). Statistics. Retrieved March 5, 2018, from https://english.mol.gov.tw/6387/

National Archives Administration. (2015). Changing population: Taiwan's family planning as a forever challenge. National Development Council, Taiwan. Retrieved June 28, 2017, from http://www.archives.gov.tw/Publish.aspx?cnid=802&p=412

National Development Council (2016). Taiwan's population projection 2016–2060. Taipei: Executive Yuan.

National Development Council (Taiwan) (2012). *Taiwan Statistical Data Book 2016*. Taipei: Executive Yuan (Taiwan).

National Statistics (Taiwan). (2016). Retrieved April 12, 2017, from http://www.stat.gov.tw/mp.asp?mp=4

National Statistics (Taiwan). (2017). Retrieved April 12, 2017, from http://www.stat.gov.tw/mp.asp?mp=4

OECD Statistics. (2017). Retrieved March 5, 2018 from http://stats.oecd.org/

Organisation for Economic Co-operation and Development (2014). *OECD Economic Survey Korea*, June. Retrieved August 15, 2016, from doi: https://doi.org/10.1787/eco_surveys-kor-2014-en

Phang, Hanam S. (2005). Demographic Dividend and Labour Force Transformation in Asia: The case of the Republic of Korea. Proceedings of the United Nations Expert Group Meeting on Social and Economic Implications of Changing Population Age Structures. Retrieved April 27, 2016, from http://www.un.org/esa/population/meetings/Proceedings_EGM_Mex_2005/phang.pdf

Statistics Korea. (2015). Social indicator in 2014. Retrieved March 5, 2018, from http://kostat.go.kr/portal/eng/pressReleases/11/4/index.board?bmode=read&bSeq=&aSeq=335111&pageNo=1&rowNum=10&navCount=10&currPg=&sTarget=title&sTxt=

Tang, K.-l. (2000). *Social welfare development in East Asia*. New York: Palgrave.

Tsai, W.-H. (2002). Modernization and the development of social welfare programs in Taiwan. In P. C. Y. Chow (Ed.), *Taiwan's modernization in global perspective* (pp. 361–377). Westport: Greenwood Publishing Group, Inc.

United Nations. (2015). World Population Ageing 2015. Retrieved March 27, 2016, from http://www.un.org/en/development/desa/population/publications/pdf/ageing/WPA2015_Report.pdf

CHAPTER 8

Conclusion

Abstract The concluding chapter brings together the main points raised in the previous chapters and provides an outlook toward future development. First, with China's industrial catchup, its role as the main engine of Taiwan and South Korea's economic growth is no longer the case. However, both countries have not yet found alternative to replace the role of China. Second, large firms have played a more important role in Taiwan and South Korea's export-led economic growth. The SMEs with greater number of domestic employment have suffered from the more globalized production network. Third, the government policies in promoting economic growth are less effective than they were during the post-war development period. The greater economic opening up has weakened the governments' role in guiding the economic development.

Keywords China's role in Taiwan and South Korea's economic growth • Large firms' contribution to economic growth • Ineffective government policies • Welfare capitalism • Economic structural changes

After WWII, the global economic center of gravity began shifting toward East Asia. The economic growth that was sustained for several decades in this region has never been seen in other parts of the world. This orderly economic growth, firstly in Japan, Newly Industrialized Economies (NIEs), New Newly Industrialized Economies (NNIEs), and then in

M.-H. Chiang, *Post-Industrial Development in East Asia*,
https://doi.org/10.1007/978-981-13-0274-9_8

China, is also a quite distinctive regional phenomenon. This kind of "ladder" leading pattern of growth (from Japan, NIEs, NNIEs, and China) has maintained the average economic performance by Asian countries at a relatively high and stable level in comparison to other regions during the past decades. Asian economic growth has largely been associated with exports. Since the 1970s, export growth in this region has been far greater than the rest of the developing world. Japan was the first to have rapidly growing exports. Subsequently, other East Asian economies also achieved very high export growth rates. This export-led development strategy created very favorable trade balances for these Asian countries.

Taiwan and South Korea are the two typical examples that successfully executed export-led economic development after WWII. As mentioned in Chap. 1, private sector efforts, effective government economic policy, and the US market opening up for foreign imports are considered as essential factors for Taiwan and South Korea's post-war economic success. However, their high economic growth based on exports encountered challenges with rising domestic production costs and growing trade protectionism from the Western countries from the latter half of the 1980s. China's economic opening up provided an opportunity for Taiwanese and Korean manufacturers to maintain their products' competitiveness with economies of scale. As such, the post-war economic growth model based on exporting final consumption goods to the US was fundamentally changed. Taiwan and South Korea have started to rely on exporting intermediate goods to China to sustain their economic growth during their post-industrial development period.

The objective of this study is to present the post-industrial development experiences in Taiwan and South Korea by examining the three factors (namely the role of private business, government policy, and foreign influence) that had contributed to Taiwan's and Korea's post-war development. In other words, this study attempts to explore whether these three factors are still relevant during the post-industrial development era. The purpose is not to distinguish which factor is more important than the other in explaining Taiwan's and South Korea's post-industrial development but to evaluate the structural changes of the three factors. More specifically, by re-examining these three factors, we aim to provide a new angle to look at the development experiences of Taiwan and South Korea.

China's Changing Role in Taiwan's and South Korea's Economic Growth

The "foreign influence" has switched from the US in the post-war development era to China in the post-industrial development era. Exporting intermediate goods to China became the main engine of economic growth for Taiwan and South Korea though US has remained the main final consumption goods destination. Nonetheless, this growth model based on exporting to China did not last long. China's role as a final assembly place for Taiwanese and Korean manufacturers has changed following its wage hike, industrial upgrading, and economic restructuring toward a more consumption-based economy. Over the past few years, while Taiwan's and Korea's exports to China have increased steadily, their imports from China have progressed even more significantly. China's technological advancement has reduced its need to import intermediate goods from Taiwan and South Korea. Instead, China is now able to provide certain intermediate goods to support Taiwan's and South Korea's domestic manufacturing production. The reverse in trade relations with China has resulted in Taiwan's and South Korea's declining trade surpluses vis-à-vis China that has supported their economic growth over the last two decades. Although some Taiwanese and Korean firms moved their manufacturing production to Southeast Asian countries, China has so far remained an important ODI and export destination for both countries. The shift of exporting intermediate goods from China to other developing countries could be a long-term process. At this development crossroad, Taiwan and South Korea have tried to secure their economic interests through signing economic agreements with China. Owing to the political inconsistency, Taiwan has only implemented early harvest program under ECFA so far. In comparison, South Korea has implemented a more comprehensive FTA with China since 2015. However, due to the slow implementation of tariff schedule, the effect of the China-South Korea FTA could be limited. Beyond the "China factor", the changing macroeconomic conditions in the world, such as the US tax cut, the development of economic regionalism, the progress of WTO trade negotiations, and so on, are essential factors affecting how Taiwan's and South Korea's economies will be developed in the future.

China's economic rise has also changed the traditional pattern of the flying geese model in which China was a follower, behind Japan, NIEs, and

NNIEs. With China's quick technological progress, the country is now considered to have exceeded many ASEAN countries and is ranked in the third row, behind only Japan and NIEs. In certain product areas, China is even in direct competition with NIEs. The changing division of labor in the regional production network means that the growth model will be transformed. However, the still large quantities of exports to China indicate that Taiwan and South Korea have not yet found an alternative market to China. In fact, even though Taiwan and South Korea can successfully shift their export dependence from China to other developing countries in the future, this may not lead to higher economic growth. The greater competition from other Chinese manufacturers could squeeze Taiwanese and Korean firms' global market share, profit margin, and export potential. A possible scenario is the coexistence of cooperation and competition with their Chinese counterparts in manufacturing production. Hence, slower economic growth is expected in the future. Indeed, with Japan in economic stagnation since two decades ago, the East Asian model of development based on exports is no longer lauded in the way it once was.

Large Companies' Greater Importance in Driving Economic Growth

During the post-industrial development period, the importance of SMEs in both countries' exports has clearly declined though they have continued to play a key role in providing domestic jobs. Instead, large firms have taken a greater share in both countries' exports even though they hired fewer people at home. The change of export driver from SMEs to large firms is particularly true in Taiwan's case. Economically, such a structural change in export from SMEs to large firms is supposed to allow the country to produce with higher efficiency and greater competitiveness in the global market. In reality however, this change has had a negative impact on the domestic economy. Due to SMEs' small profits, they are not able to provide workers with remuneration at the level provided by the large companies. A large number of workers at SMEs thus received less salary than the small number of workers working at large firms. The income inequality gap has enlarged as a result. This explains partially why many people in Taiwan and South Korea do not feel that the benefits of economic growth have been well distributed. The growth in production value has been greater than the average growth in wages. The wage difference between large firms and SMEs is especially obvious in South Korea.

The majority of Taiwan and Korean SMEs are in services sector. When many Taiwanese and Korean firms invested massively abroad, domestic laborers shifted to service jobs with inferior wages. Only a small number of people are qualified for the high-value-added jobs with higher remuneration at home. Relocating labor-intensive production abroad is supposed to allow domestic industries to upgrade. However, the high unemployment rate for the highly educated youth indicates that both countries are not creating enough number of high-value-added jobs at home after relocation of factories abroad. The slow progress of wages in Taiwan and Korea could also imply that the companies are having difficulties in global market competition. In other words, they have to rely on lower wages at home to maintain their export competitiveness rather than through innovation and technological development.

Large firms' growing ODI drove their massive exports to developing countries. In other words, large firms have benefited from expanding their business abroad while domestic workers have suffered from the economic globalization over the last two decades. While wages for employees at SMEs have progressed insignificantly, the wealthy have become richer. The rising housing prices have aggregated the income inequality issue. Soaring real estate prices reflect heavy speculation in these assets which widens the wealth gap between asset holders and regular workers.

Large firms have become more dominant in both economies but the business operation model is still different. Over the last two decades, Taiwan's production relations with global MNCs have transformed from a group of SMEs with production flexibility to a few large firms. While Taiwan has developed a few large companies in making components or doing final assembly for large MNCs, South Korea's chaebols have been able to integrate upstream, midstream, and downstream manufacturing processes. For example, the Taiwan Semiconductor Manufacturing Company (TSMC) is the global top IC foundry and Hon Hai is the top subcontractor for Apple. They are important component suppliers and product makers for global MNCs' branded products. Meanwhile, some of Taiwan's SMEs act as satellite companies in supporting large firms' production needs at home. In comparison, Korea's Samsung has built up a comprehensive production line. They are in direct competition with other MNCs in the global markets for the branded ICT products. However, the integration between SMEs and large chaebols in manufacturing production is less obvious in South Korea.

Ineffective Government Policies in Promoting Economic Growth During the Post-Industrial Development Period

During the post-industrial development period, both governments have tried to revive the "state-led development model" in the hope of regaining high economic growth. In reality, however, the governments have not been able to reverse the trend of economic slowdown. Democratization is often considered to be an important reason for the waning role of states in economic development. In 1987, Taiwan lifted martial law and South Korea also held its first direct presidential election. Democratization introduced competitive politics which challenged the bureaucrats' absolute power in economic policymaking. Economic liberalization has further exposed the two economies to influence from the global environment. In particular, South Korea has liberalized its market furthermore after the AFC. In comparison, Taiwan's government was more cautious about the flow of international capital. Still, Taiwan has tried to open up its economy in order to adapt to the globalization trend and to engage in various global economic activities. In the last decade, the development of economic regionalism has pushed the two countries to actively get involved in both bilateral and multilateral FTA negotiations. Nevertheless, the greater involvement in the global economy seems to have eroded the capacity and autonomy of the state vis-à-vis non-state actors.

In fact, it can be argued that the state has never been an important driver for the economic development. Instead, Taiwan's and South Korea's post-war economic successes are a result of the governments' policy consistency to the global economic trends. For example, during the post-war development period, the Taiwanese and Korean governments' export promotion policy was aligned with the US market opening up for foreign imports. Trade liberalization was in response to the protectionism from the Western countries. The Taiwanese government relaxed the rules for investment in China because of the unstoppable "China fever". In other words, the governments' policymaking has been from a passive position rather than active pursuit of economic objectives. During the post-industrial development period, the two governments have further enacted greater deregulation in trade and investment in order to cope with globalization. Nevertheless, the policy consistency to the global economic trend during the post-industrial development period does not help to promote economic growth. Both countries have experienced economic slowdown.

Both have considered economic liberalization as a necessity for promoting economic growth and competition and deregulation have been emphasized. As such, they have tried to engage in all kinds of FTAs with different economies in the world. Unlike Korea, Taiwan's limited diplomatic space has constrained its capacity in launching FTA negotiations with other countries. Nonetheless, South Korea's FTAs with several economies has not appeared to be a significant driver for economic growth either. Its merchandise trade surplus has increased but its service trade deficit has enlarged. The greater involvement in the global free trade network seems to have enhanced South Korea's comparative advantage in manufacturing production. However, the uncompetitive services sector did not benefit. Overall, the two economies did not grow as much as expected following the greater economic liberalization.

Another important policy measure during the post-industrial development period is the industrial upgrading policy. Industrial upgrading is considered essential for promoting economic growth. However, the government's intervention in industrial upgrading is not always useful. In Taiwan's case, the government's promotion of the "Two Trillion and Twin Star Development Program" proved a failure due to the insufficient R&D expenditure for its long-term development. In South Korea, chaebols have played a more important role in developing the country's R&D capacity. The government's push for an "innovation-driven" economy has reinforced chaebols' importance in the economy. Despite the efforts to implement industrial upgrading policy measures, Taiwan and South Korea are still relying on foreign technology, notably from the US and Japan. The two countries' relatively small economic sizes have limited their governments' capacity to spend on R&D. As such, compared with China, Taiwan's and South Korea's total R&D expenditure has been lagging behind since about a decade ago. Another important aspect in industrial upgrading is the effort to develop high-value-added services. Over the last few decades, Taiwan's and South Korea's services sector have been mostly low-value-added and non-tradable. The effect of promoting services sectors' development has been limited so far.

Moving Toward Welfare Capitalism

Like Japan, Taiwan, and South Korea also have rapidly aging populations and shrinking labor forces. Driven by such demographics, economic growth in both countries is expected to slow down even more.

Accompanying the slower economic growth is the potential unsustainability of government expenditure for the growing aging population in need of social benefits. The policy measures in the last two decades to encourage birth do not seem effective as evidenced by the continual falling TFR. The proposed measures in this book such as raising productivity, encouraging female and youth labor participation and greater deregulation for foreign laborers could alleviate the challenges in the short to medium term. However, aging population is a long-term trend. The policy measures to cope with the challenges from an aging population will have to be wider in scope and greater in expenditure. Aging population and growing social welfare expenditure is hence another important factor in guiding the future development of Taiwan and South Korea toward welfare capitalism.

Welfare capitalism in both countries can be traced back to a few decades ago. Taiwan's and South Korea's welfare capitalism system was built by conservative elites in the absence of competitive politics. The welfare benefits were granted to those considered important to the governments (Fleckenstein & Lee, 2017). From the 1950s to the 1970s, the social welfare policy development in Taiwan and South Korea was initiated mainly for political reasons rather than to simply meet welfare needs. As mentioned in Chap. 7, both countries had introduced social benefits for their targeted groups as a "preemptive strike" to compensate for the regimes' lack of political legitimacy. The orientation of social policy only underwent fundamental change in the 1980s when the grassroots movements started to develop in Taiwan and South Korea, as part of struggles for democracy. The opposition party in Taiwan put social policy on the election campaign agenda against the ruling KMT. To maintain their political legitimacy, the KMT government was forced to respond with rising advocacy for the social welfare to be extended to the general public. In South Korea, the rapid economic growth during the 1970s and 1980s did not promote growing welfare spending from the government. The full employment rate and satisfaction with the high economic growth could have enabled people to tolerate self-financing of welfare expenses. However, the end of the high economic growth era and wage stagnation has made social welfare spending an increasing burden for the general public. The large number of unemployed people after the AFC was a wakeup call to the Korean government and people on the importance of social insurance. A comprehensive social policy and welfare expenditure came to be considered imperative for social stability.

Over the last decade, when Taiwan and South Korea started to experience shocking low TFR, the countries' welfare policies have been aiming to encourage birth and to increase social responsibility for the elderly.

Economic growth has been emphasized as it is an important pillar to support rising welfare expenditure. Some have argued that the welfare policy and economic development policy are mutually supportive. While economic growth helps to finance social welfare expenditure, economic development can also be energized by social policy which has helped to enhance labor productivity, encourage enterprises training and subsidized wages, among other benefits (Holliday & Wilding, 2003).

With Taiwan and South Korea gradually becoming more involved in the global economy, their motivations for developing welfare policy are not only from domestic factors but also from global influences. Globalization, an integration process driven chiefly by trade and investment, is supposed to increase the welfare of all people worldwide. In reality however, not everyone has benefited from globalization. Small companies and less competitive sectors in a country often suffer from foreign competition while large competitive firms are able to expand their business in this globalized world. Hence, some have argued that globalization has facilitated capital outflow so as to avoid high taxation (Holliday & Wilding, 2003). This could be true. It is widely reported in recent years that many Taiwanese and Korean entrepreneurs have invested in "tax havens", including the Cayman Islands, the Virgin Islands, Bermuda, and so on, so as to retain their profits. The rapid rise of direct investment to tax havens has become a problem for governments as this investment is mainly for the purpose of dodging taxes. On the other hand, some have argued that globalization has helped governments to develop a more comprehensive social protection system to protect their citizens from the impact of globalization (Holliday & Wilding 2003, p. 163). Although welfare measures have been put into practice to help the small businesses and laborers in vulnerable sectors, the enlarging income inequality indicates that the impact from globalization has outpaced the benefits received from the governments.

The issue of aging population undoubtedly poses the most critical challenge to the development of social policy in Taiwan and South Korea. Taiwan has implemented National Annuity since 2008 with the aim to provide steady income for the aged. As it is not compulsory, many people choose to not be included in the National Annuity. Indeed, compared with the potentially large medical expense, the small income from the National Annuity after retirement may not be much helpful. It is estimated that the elderly in Taiwan would become disabled for about 8–12 years before their demise. The official statistics show that current disabled aging people accounted for 17 percent of the total aging population. Therefore, the more important thing is to provide a comprehensive long-term care services system for the growing aging population. Similarly in South Korea, medical expenses have become the most important expenditure for the elderly. However, the social safety net is not good enough to cover that expenditure. Pressures to create more new schemes to improve the current social welfare program for the elderly would only become more considerable in the foreseeable future.

In sum, the improving global economy will continue to support Taiwan and South Korea's export-led economic recovery in the short term. Taiwan's close production relations with their counterparts in China and large multinational firms in the US will remain essential for sustaining its economic growth. South Korean chaebols' greater and more diversified international business is the main source of the country's economic growth. South Korea's relatively higher government expenditure has made its outperformed Taiwan's economic growth rate in the last few years. However, the long-term economic prospect is very uncertain. Taiwan and South Korea are facing similar challenges during the post-industrial development era though their macroeconomic performance is slightly different. The China factor, large firms' greater dominance in the economy, trend of globalization, growing gap between the rich and the poor, and growing aging population in both countries have posed the utmost challenges to the future economic growth. Nevertheless, the government policies so far are not able to successfully solve all these challenges. This is not to suggest the government policy is not important but the medicine for the economic illness may not be right. Indeed, those above-mentioned challenges signify a new growth model needs to be constructed. Both countries will have to find alternative for exports other than China, balance the economic structure between large and small firms, and provide friendly business environment for nurturing competitive emerging firms. Economic growth is imperative in the face of rising expending for the upcoming aging societies. The pro-active intervention is imperative for ensuring a more sustainable development.

References

Fleckenstein, T., & Lee, S. C. (2017). Democratization, post-industrialization and East Asian welfare capitalism: the politics of welfare state reform in Japan, South Korea and Taiwan. *Journal of International and Comparative Social Policy., 33*(1), 36–54.

Holliday, I., & Wilding, P. (2003). Conclusion. In I. Holloday & P. Wilding (Eds.), *Welfare capitalism in East Asia: Social policy in the tiger economies.* Hampshire and New York: Palgrave Macmillan.

Index

M.-H. Chiang, *Post-Industrial Development in East Asia*,
https://doi.org/10.1007/978-981-13-0274-9

F

G

H

I

K

L

M

The manufacturer's authorised representative in the EU is Springer Nature Customer Service Centre GmbH, Europaplatz 3, 69115 Heidelberg, Germany. If you have any concerns regarding our products, please contact ProductSafety@springernature.com

Printed and bound by CPI Group (UK) Ltd, Croydon, CR0 4YY
25/09/2026
02222897-0018